extended project

STUDENT GUIDE

extended project

innovate ✳
create ✳✳
succeed ✳✳

Brian Crossland
Patrick Walsh-Atkins

STUDENT GUIDE

HODDER
EDUCATION
AN HACHETTE UK COMPANY

Orders: please contact Bookpoint Ltd, 130 Milton Park, Abingdon, Oxon OX14 4SB. Telephone: (44) 01235 827720. Fax: (44) 01235 400454. Lines are open from 9.00 – 5.00, Monday to Saturday, with a 24-hour message answering service. You can also order through our website www.hoddereducation.co.uk.

British Library Cataloguing in Publication Data
A catalogue record for this title is available from the British Library

ISBN: 978 1 444 102 260

First Published 2009
Impression number 10 9 8 7 6 5 4 3 2 1
Year   2015 2014 2013 2012 2011 2010 2009

Cover photo © Image 100 Ltd
Typeset by Transet Limited, Coventry, England.
Printed in Great Britain for Hodder Education, part of Hachette UK, 338 Euston Road, London NW1 3BH by MPG Books, Bodmin.

Contents

Acknowledgments

The authors and publisher wish to thank OCR for their kind permission to use copyright materials in this book.

What is the Level 3 Extended Project?

Learning goals

By the end of this chapter you should be able to:

- Identify the requirements of the Extended Project
- Start thinking about a topic for your Extended Project.

The Level 3 Extended Project (EP) is a substantial piece of work which has the following features:

- The topic is chosen by you, the student.
- The project can be submitted in a variety of different formats (outcomes).
- It is completed by you, largely on your own, with some support and supervision.
- Completing the project enables you to develop and demonstrate a wide range of skills which are highly rated by prospective employers and in higher education.

Extended Projects are usually completed over the course of a year or more, with the school/college providing basic training in some of the key skills required, such as:

- project management
- planning
- research
- presentation
- review and evaluation.

Schools and colleges will also give you a degree of support and supervision to enable you to succeed in your chosen project. As a student you have an entitlement to initial teaching and preparation, as well as ongoing supervision while you undertake the project. Schools and colleges are expected to provide the framework for you to do your chosen project, but not actually to do it for you.

Some recent successful projects have included:

- designing and building a steam engine
- a critical study of D. H. Lawrence
- an investigation into media bias

Moderator's hint
Make sure that you make full use of both the training and supervision provided, as they are vital to your success.

- making a documentary film
- managing an event
- researching family history.

The preceding list will give you some idea of the range of things you could do. Simply downloading material from the Internet or reworking A Level work may seem an easy option but is not a recipe for success; in fact, such attempts have failed to make the grade. A successful Project might fit into and progress on from your current studies, or it might just be something that interests you and has nothing to do with your courses at all.

The Extended Project gives you an opportunity to:

Moderator's hint
Some EPs are linked to A Levels, but most are not.

- demonstrate skills and abilities outside the normal examination framework
- learn a whole range of further skills, such as project management, which will be invaluable to your further education, higher education and working life
- demonstrate to yourself, your family, your teachers, universities/HE institutions and future employers what you can achieve on your own
- show that you have enterprise, initiative and self-motivation
- explore in detail and depth a subject which interests you personally
- move outside the often narrow area of your A Levels/Diploma
- earn some valuable UCAS points
- gather real evidence for your UCAS personal statement, UCAS interview, or interview for employment, of what you can do and have achieved
- prove that you have got what it takes to achieve a first class degree/complete a job, with minimal supervision.

Some of the skills that you will have gained at GCSE/A Level/through your Level 1 or 2 Projects (such as communication) will be very useful while working on your Extended Project. However, the key word here is 'extended'. You need to show clearly that you can move on and extend yourself from GCSE/A Level/Diploma; it is your chance to show that you are more than just a good geographer/sports scientist etc.

The Extended Project and progression to work or university

Learning goals

By the end of the chapter you should be able to:

- Describe the links between the Extended Project and future studies
- Identify the commitment required to progress into work or university.

Employers, universities and other forms of higher education support the purpose of the Extended Project and value it highly, for the following reasons:

- In any kind of employment or further training, such as an apprenticeship, the ability to research new topics and areas of interest is vital.
- The skills that the Extended Project requires are vital for success in higher education.
- A Level students are often spoon-fed material, with success depending too much on excellent teaching. If you are spoon-fed for your project, you will fail. Universities/HE institutions do not spoon-feed; they want to see students who can achieve on their own. The EP shows so well what a potential student can do on their own.
- A Level can be just a measure of achievement whereas the Extended Project can indicate your potential.
- It can demonstrate real commitment towards a subject, which admissions tutors are looking for when selecting students for courses in high demand.
- Your achievement at university is largely down to you; this is exactly the same for the Extended Project.
- Employers will also appreciate other skills which you will have developed through the Extended Project, including planning, focusing on a subject, selecting documents for a purpose, communications and presentation

The EP can not only help you get into HE, but can also enable you to do well there. Put yourself in the position of an admissions tutor of a medical school. You are faced with two candidates, X and Y, who both have:

- strong support from their UCAS referee
- good AS grades and A Level forecast grades
- well-crafted personal statements.

However, whereas X's personal statement is similar to that of many other hopeful medics, Y's statement is quite different as she has done an Extended Project on 'Hospices and Hospice Care'. This involved a considerable amount of her time and effort, and she did a lot of practical work and observation in local hospices as part of her project. She deservedly gained a high grade, and this work was a key factor in her decision to study medicine.

In order to succeed in a field, you need a real and lasting commitment to the subject as well as skills and knowledge. The Extended Project is a superb way of demonstrating this commitment, and many of the other qualities that admissions tutors want to see. In this example, Y could be the favoured candidate as:

- there is evidence that she will not drop out of her course and thus deprive another of a valued place (and potentially waste taxpayers' money)
- she is well aware of what life is like at the 'rough' end of medicine
- she has demonstrated real commitment
- she is more than just a good scientist.

 PUTTING INTO PRACTICE

The scenario above is just one of the many examples where the EP can play a key role in entry to university courses in high demand. Other examples are given in Table 1. ● ● ●

Project area	Course
Investigation into magistrates' courts	Law/London
Sport coaching in primary schools	Sports College/Exeter
Writing a play in French	Modern Languages/Oxbridge
Computer software design	Maths/Oxbridge

Table 1 Examples of Extended Projects which led to university admission

Few universities make an offer based on an EP grade as it is not yet available to all students, but they do value the skills gained by completing it.

The Extended Project and the Diploma

Learning goals

By the end of the chapter you should be able to:

- Identify the relationships between the project and your current studies
- Develop an overview of the Extended Project requirements
- Identify broad areas of interest for your choice of topic.

If you are studying for a Diploma at Advanced Level, an Extended Project is a compulsory part of the whole Diploma course. The rules are slightly different for Diploma students from those for students who are doing the Extended Project as a standalone course. The rubric states that as part of a Diploma, candidates will be able to show:

- how the Extended Project **complements** and **develops** the theme and topics of the Principal Learning (e.g. ICT)
  and/or
- how it supports **progression**.

This gives the Diploma student a lot of scope, but not quite as much freedom as the student on a standalone course.

To succeed as a Diploma student, the following points are important in shaping your Extended Project:

- Stay within the broad area of your Diploma if you possibly can.
- Come up with your own ideas for a topic within the Line of Learning before you become pressurised into doing something which does not interest you.
- If there is something you really want to explore but it seems to be outside the area of learning of your Diploma, see if you can argue a case that it 'supports progression'. It may be that you are interested in genealogy/family history and doing the ICT Diploma, so why not develop a database which could link the two? OCR interprets the phrase 'supports progression' quite broadly, so if in doubt, ask your supervisor to approach OCR for advice.
- Always remember that your project will be judged on the skills you display during the course of working on it.

Table 2 gives examples of Extended Projects chosen by Diploma students which successfully integrated their own interests with the need to demonstrate skills and cover relevant subject matter.

Engineering students	ICT students	Creative/media students
A dissertation on Brunel	Designing a computer-aided/controlled lighting design for a performance	A report on media bias
Designing a hydraulic system	Designing a programme	Making a film
Investigating stress in materials	Investigating the causes of major software project failures	Writing and directing a play
Making locks	A dissertation on software development	A dissertation on Joe Orton

Table 2 Topics for Extended Projects chosen by Diploma students

Reasons for doing the Extended Project

If you are given a choice of doing the Extended Project or something else such as General Studies, consider the following points in favour of the Extended Project:

- It is valuable when applying for HE.
- It is of relevance to the world of work.
- You will gain valuable skills which you can transfer to many areas of employment and HE.
- You can prove that you are more than an average student.
- You can give evidence of your initiative.
- It allows you to show that you have real commitment to your subject area.

Choosing a topic and a title

Learning goals

By the end of the chapter you should be able to:

- Select a range of topics
- Focus on a topic which is of interest to you
- Ensure that your choice of topic provides opportunities to achieve a high score.

This can be one of the most important stages of the whole Extended Project. The first vital step is to decide on the **broad** area to work on. Do not worry about a definite title at this stage, as that can wait until much later. Some very successful projects only decided on the final wording of the title at the very end.

HOW TO SUCCEED

Decide on a broad topic first.

Choosing the topic

What works as a good topic for the Extended Project? There is no easy answer to this one, but here are some basic rules to consider:

- Start with something which really interests you; this is vital. It could be anything, from the musical ability of Paul McCartney to modern yacht design or one of your grandparent's experiences in 'care' in the 1940s. All of these ideas have led to successful projects.
- Do not worry about what others may think of your idea. Most successful projects begin with a rather vague idea about something that interests the student. One skateboard enthusiast did an excellent project on skateboard design and manufacture, and went on to university to study Product Design.
- Check with your supervisor about how possible he or she thinks it will be, particularly in terms of research.
- You will be spending a lot of time on this project, so it should be something that really interests you. You will also be interviewed on it by your examiners, a lay and specialist audience, possibly employers or

university admissions tutors, and any of those could easily spot whether or not your interest is genuine.

- Remember that it is a chance to display skills and show what you can do on your own. You are most likely to do that if your personal interest and motivation is driving the project.
- Think about the way in which the project is marked and assessed; how well will it fit into the criteria? Remember that no one will expect you to provide the final answer on your subject, but if you have shown clearly while dealing with this topic that you can plan, design, research, develop, realise and finally review it, you have chosen a good area.
- You can choose a topic which is closely linked in 'subject' terms to your other studies (be it A Levels, Diploma, B Tech, Nationals, etc.), provided it is something which really interests you, demonstrates 'progression on' from those studies, does not form a part of those studies, and fits into the assessment criteria by which the Extended Project is marked.
- Resist any pressure to do something which will for example help your A level in French/your Diploma in ICT/look good on your CV/UCAS form, etc. If you are not really interested, then choose something else.
- Keep it fairly broad to start with. For example, 'I would like to do something about the Punjab/computer games programming' is quite a good way to set out, as you can always narrow the topic down and convert it into something that works.
- Do not start with too narrow a focus. 'I would like to teach a lesson on the Holocaust' was a topic suggested by a student, but did not appear to offer much scope for research and planning, etc. However, broadened out into a much wider topic of 'Why and how topics such as the Holocaust should be taught' this might form an excellent project as it offers a real chance to develop the required skills.
- Avoid something where you are going to need an enormous amount of help. You have to do this project largely on your own. You can ask for guidance and expert advice/opinions, but self-reliance is the key. Do not depend totally on others; this applies to an individual project as well as a group project.

HOW TO SUCCEED

Many of the higher grade projects were praised for 'the tremendous independence shown' – so show it!

- If the basic idea is for example to make a film with two or three others, make sure that the individual roles are clearly identifiable, such as who will direct, produce, write the script, etc.

Ask yourself the following questions before deciding on your topic for the Extended Project:

1 Does it really interest me?
2 Can I get it to work?
3 Can I achieve an A* by meeting the assessment criteria?
4 Can I do it largely on my own?
5 If it is part of a group, can **my** work still be identified and assessed if the others drop out or do not achieve highly?

Choosing the title

Resist all pressure to make any decision about the final title too early. Very often your research may lead you in a very different direction to the one you first thought of. Your initial idea for a topic may have been 'Set design in the theatre'. At least three students started with that idea in mind, yet their final projects finished as:

- designing and building a set for 'Cabaret' (an artefact)
- set design for Shakespeare (a dissertation)
- the training of set designers (a report).

Moderator's hint
Always keep the possible title under review and be prepared to change it.

Take for example the basic idea of 'something to do with MRSA'. This topic was considered because the student:

1 was taking biology and chemistry A Levels or a related Diploma
2 was considering a career/HE course in medicine or a related area
3 had a relative who nearly died of it.

MRSA is a vast topic which would need to be narrowed down, but as there was a real interest there and the supervisor could see how this could fit into the project assessment criteria, it went ahead.

This project offered lots of scope:

- for planning
- for research, using a wide variety of sources from researchers, people working to prevent its spread, sufferers, textbooks, media, etc.
- as it lent itself well to a report/investigation

Moderator's hint
When thinking about both topic and title, always consider how marks are allocated.

- as it was straightforward when it came to review and the presentation
- for the student to demonstrate her interest and ability.

Initial research was then done with a possible title being 'The causes and spread of MRSA'. However, about a third of the way through the time allocated, during a regular review session with her supervisor, it became clear that this would not quite meet the criteria, and there was a real risk of getting bogged down in the technical description of what MRSA was. The title changed to 'Why has MRSA proved so difficult to combat?'

Guidelines for choosing your title

- Start off with a broad idea; do not worry about the title too early.
- Do some serious research on your chosen topic.
- Try to narrow it down by the midway review at the latest.
- Be prepared to change the title.
- Be prepared to change the format.
- Stop to think whether it will still fit the assessment criteria when you make any changes.
- Make sure you note carefully the reasons for changing your approach/format/direction/title, as that could be a critical part of the review process (AO4).

The review of the successful projects in 2008 suggested that if you were doing a dissertation, then posing a question such as 'Why was Winston Churchill unsuccessful as a peacetime Prime Minister?' was more likely to bring success than 'Winston Churchill as peacetime Prime Minister', but this did not apply to a production/artefact, etc.

In the end the title is not so important (and this is where it can differ from coursework); what matters is whether you are planning, designing, researching, developing and reviewing, as this is where the marks are awarded. Several very successful projects were given titles only at the last minute.

Keep your supervisor briefed on what is happening as far as title and overall direction is concerned. Their questioning of your reasons for changing can be vital for assessment.

Often there is pressure on moderators when talking to teachers and students to give a list of successful titles. They tend to resist that as the key reason why a project (and not the title) worked was because of the efforts of the student (and the quality of their teachers/supervisors), and not because of the title itself. However, the following are just some of the project areas which achieved high grades in the review, which give an idea of the range. There is scope for plenty more:

- making a dress modelled on the designs and techniques of Dior's 'New Look'
- human rights for refugees
- the novels of Mary Shelley
- business plan for barn conversions
- solar variability and cloud cover
- Fair Trade
- surgery and cosmetic defects
- animation using 3D models
- bereavement
- performance: Elton John
- magnetic levitation
- organic farming
- the NHS and its portrayal in the media
- Islamophobia
- Irish folk music
- equestrian events
- Picasso
- an investigation into paracetamol
- a fanzine
- Catholic teaching on euthanasia

Project formats

You need to produce an outcome for your Extended Project which should be either a design, a performance, a report, a dissertation or an artefact. These outcomes fall into four broad suggested formats. They are:

■ a dissertation
■ a report or investigation
■ a production
■ an artefact.

Your project may not fall neatly into one of these types, and may be a mixture of two. Students working in a group might want to offer different formats, with one doing a production and another a dissertation. This is permissible, as OCR allows the mixing of formats.

A dissertation

This should be about 5,000 words, but do not worry if it is slightly over or under this number. It may contain maps, diagrams, data and illustrations if necessary. You may have appendices if you wish, but they should be of real importance and should not form more than 20 per cent of the total. Do not use appendices to show off a list of facts you have discovered which do not add anything to the project in terms of your skills.

> **Moderator's hint**
> You can combine formats if you wish, such as part-artefact and part-report.

A dissertation should contain:

■ an introduction
■ a table of contents with page references
■ the main body of the dissertation
■ any works cited listed in a bibliography (which may have comments on the value of the resources used. They need not necessarily only be written sources, as interviews could be an equally important resource).

There is a separate section in the book on how to write a dissertation, but remember that your skills are being assessed (such as planning and evaluation), so always bear that in mind and do not become carried away by the content. If for example you are taking geography A Level and want to do a dissertation on some aspect of human geography which really interests you, this is allowed provided it is a clear **extension** of that learning and not just old coursework reworked. Your supervisor will advise you on this issue.

Moderator's hint
You may do a project on some aspect of Physics if you are doing Physics A Level, but it must clearly be an 'extension' of your A Level studies.

Factors which lead to successful dissertations

Do not treat the project as a conventional piece of coursework. Remember, content itself is not marked. The project will be judged on your ability to do the following successfully:

- Manage a project, thinking of a broad topic and a title (in that order), planning and preparing for the project, acquiring new skills (research, data use, etc.) (20 per cent of the marks).
- Use sensibly and think critically about a wide range of resources – not just a couple of text books and Wikipedia (20 per cent of the marks).

Moderator's hint
Moderators are looking for evidence of a wide range of resources.

- Develop and realise: this means writing the dissertation after you have completed the research, checking it carefully and submitting it on time. You must give your school/college time to assess it properly (40 per cent of the marks).
- Review the whole project. Demonstrate clearly that you have continuously reflected on what you have done. Did you change title? Did you change format? Did you change the focus of the project? If so, why? On reflection was it a good idea? What would you do better next time? What have you learned to do or avoid doing? (20 per cent of the marks).

You should keep good records of all aspects of the project, not just notes taken for the 'content' part. Remember that the **content** itself is not the most important thing; marks are awarded for demonstrating skills.

Successful dissertations

- are based on something that interests you personally
- are based on a hypothesis or question, e.g. 'How successful was Winston Churchill as Chancellor of the Exchequer?', rather than 'The cause of

the collapse of Northern Rock'. The latter type can end up as tedious lists which do not demonstrate your skills
- are not done because they might be useful for your A Level/Diploma and were suggested by someone else. They are done because **you** want to work on that topic
- demonstrate your own enterprise and initiative, planning and project management skills, not just your willingness to sit in a library and read books.

Less successful dissertations

- are weighed down in detail and focused on content – like coursework
- provide little evidence of the skills for which marks are awarded, such as planning
- are obviously reworked parts of the A Level course
- have a limited range of resources used: just a couple of textbooks and Wikipedia
- are done in the wrong format; a dissertation instead of a report
- have no review/evaluation.

Moderator's hint
The dissertation can often seem to be the easy option when thinking about formats for your project, but it can be the hardest format in which to demonstrate skills.

A report or investigation

This should also be about 5,000 words, with allowances for data, statistics, etc. If required, the data/results can be a part of the word count. No one is going to count the words. If you use a lot less, but have a lot of key data which you have organised (as opposed to just downloaded), then that is fine. The possible range of reports/investigations is enormous, for example:

- comparing provision for disabled people among different local authorities
- advanced geography fieldwork
- MPs' expenses
- media coverage of certain types of events
- business methods.

Key to success here is to choose an issue which interests you, is manageable and accessible, has accessible resources, gives you scope to achieve high marks, and lends itself to this format.

HOW TO SUCCEED

Making sure that resources are available can be essential for a report/investigation.

The report/investigation will be judged on your ability to do the following:

- Manage a project; your ability to plan will be vital here.
- Use critically a wide range of different resources, such as interviews, published data as well as secondary sources, different types of media, etc.
- Collate the information and ideas gained from those resources effectively.
- Deliver a finished product in a comprehensible form, on time.
- Review effectively what you have done. What worked? What did not work? Why? What have you learned? What would you do better next time? What would you not do again? Why?

Successful reports/investigations:

> **Moderator's hint**
> Poor planning and limited resources are often the main reasons for awarding low marks for reports.

- are clearly written by well-motivated students who felt strongly about the subject
- demonstrate very obviously the planning skills and enterprise of the student
- take very seriously the requirement to use a wide range of resources and to evaluate critically. There should be plenty of comments such as 'This interview was very useful because....' or 'This information came from a very biased source as ...'
- have a clear conclusion based on solid evidence
- show a real willingness to reflect on the whole process and learn for the future.

Less successful reports:

- look suspiciously like material required for other exams
- show poor planning as insufficient time was left to use key resources
- discover too late that a key resource was unavailable
- take on too big a topic, or too limited a topic which gives too little scope to demonstrate the required skills
- never reach a conclusion
- lack evaluation (the most frequent reason for low marks).

An artefact

This could be something you have made or designed. The possible range is vast: it could be artwork, a costume for a play, a working model, an educational game. It could be a design or a series of designs; the whole idea is to give you the maximum scope possible. If in any doubt about the format, contact your awarding body about it. There have been cases where the student was discouraged from doing an artefact because their school or college was worried about the student going into areas beyond the experience/expertise of the supervisors and the college. Usually these worries were totally unnecessary.

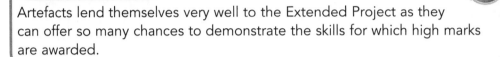

HOW TO SUCCEED

Artefacts lend themselves very well to the Extended Project as they can offer so many chances to demonstrate the skills for which high marks are awarded.

Successful artefacts have included the following:

- a dress
- sculpture
- computer programs
- building designs
- steam engines.

You will need to submit a written report with your artefact, at about 1,500 words. Some of those words may be in the form of a commentary on different parts of the designs. No one is going to count the words carefully if you are clearly meeting the assessment criteria. You can use this report to meet the AO1, AO2 and AO4 criteria, demonstrating the following skills:

1 Planning: for example, how you anticipated problems, obtained the right resources at the right time.
2 Critically using the 'wide range of resources'.
3 Reviewing and evaluating.

HOW TO SUCCEED

Make sure that your report allows you to achieve marks for managing, researching and evaluating.

AO3 should be covered by the artefact itself.

Your artefact will be judged on your ability to do the following:

- Manage the whole project, from the initial idea stage through to completion. Strong evidence of your planning will be critical here.
- Use a wide range of resources critically. The resources could range from interviews through to the designs of other artefacts, or secondary and primary sources. The potential list is vast and the type of resources will depend very largely on the nature of the project.
- Complete the artefact in a specified time. There have been cases where the actual artefact has not been completed but there was enough evidence (such as photographic) of the process for marks to be gained.
- Review and evaluate the whole process. What worked? Why? What did not? Why not? What was learned? What would or would not be repeated next time?

EVIDENCE
Good evidence of detailed planning and use of a wide range of resources is vital for success with artefacts.

Successful artefact-based projects:

- are well planned (good planning is perhaps more important and a greater challenge in this format than in the others)
- involve the anticipation and learning of necessary skills (for example, arc welding, reading French)
- demonstrate the individuality and enterprise of the student
- reach outside the conventional educational 'box'
- have a high level of review and evaluation.

Less successful artefact-based projects:

- have bright ideas but bad planning
- do not achieve the timescale
- discover too late that the acquisition of a certain skill is vital to complete the project
- do not think through the transition from the bright idea to actual artefact
- expect too much help from others.

A production

Moderator's hint
Do not be frightened about going down the artefact route; it can lead to brilliant projects.

As with the other formats, there is a huge range of possibilities here. It could be a play, a film, a concert, a DVD, an event. Again, if you are not sure, contact OCR for advice.

Remember what it is being assessed: if your planning, researching, evaluation, etc. is perfect, but you forget your lines in the performance of a play which you have written and in which you have the lead role, marks will not necessarily be deducted (although you might want to reflect on your line-learning skills and how to deal with pressure for AO4!).

This project format will be judged on your ability to do the following:

- Plan the production: did you allow sufficient time to rehearse?
- Use a wide range of resources critically.
- Deliver the production.
- Reflect and evaluate on the whole process. What went well, and why? What did not, and why? What would you do better next time?

HOW TO SUCCEED

Do not concentrate too much on the production itself; remember it is a way of demonstrating your skills.

Successful productions:

- manage to translate the bright idea into an actual production without harming the essential 'creativity' behind it
- are realistic, downsizing as necessary
- remember the assessment criteria: a stunning piece of film-making or music-writing will not achieve an A grade without the production demonstrating your planning, investigation and evaluation skills
- take the written report seriously. It should not be a rushed afterthought which neglects evidence of your skills. The production itself does not always display the skills required, particularly to a lay audience.

Less successful productions:

- do not actually happen: the idea simply does not translate into practice
- forget what is being assessed. You might be the next Steven Spielberg, but if there is no evidence of planning or no report you will not gain high marks
- lack evidence of planning and resource use. If you are writing a play then you must still demonstrate your research and evaluation skills
- become the vehicle for one person's ego, or disintegrate over personality clashes
- do not provide evidence of individual contributions and skills within a group production.

Working in a group

Remember the rules for group productions (see the next chapter – Group Extended Projects).

Changing formats

If you decide halfway through your project that you want to change format, for example that a dissertation would be better presented as a report, this is permissible. The end product is the one which will be assessed. You need to keep a proper record of the reasons for the change however, as that will be important for both your AO1 and AO4 marks.

Group Extended Projects

Learning goals

By the end of the chapter you should be able to:

- Work within a team, recording your individual progress
- Identify suitable evidencing techniques.

A group may decide to work together for their projects. There is no objection to this at all from OCR, and there have been some very successful groups in the past, but check with your awarding body. Working successfully in a group is a very important skill to acquire and will gain high marks.

Groups have worked successfully together and produced projects such as:

- dissertations: involving historical research
- reports/investigations: examining media bias
- artefacts: designing and making different sets/costumes/props for different parts of a play
- productions: different roles in film-making or in creating a business.

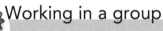

Working in a group

Groups can complete their projects in any format or mix of formats.

What is vital is that each member of the group remembers that they must provide evidence to demonstrate **their own** planning, research, evaluation, etc, as well as their contribution to the group as a whole. Keeping very careful records is perhaps more important here than with other projects. Groups can for example work on different aspects of an investigation. There is no need for the group to all submit in the same format; for example a group of three students may be involved in a play where:

- one person writes the play (the play is submitted with a report)
- another person directs the play and is the lead actor (a DVD of a performance plus a written report is submitted)
- the third person does all the design and production for the play (a mixture of the artefacts and a report is submitted).

When executed in this way, it is easier to identify and assess the individual contributions of each student. Like so many other aspects of the Extended Project, groups will work successfully if there is sensible planning and regular review.

Working in a group

Remember the critical importance of keeping evidence of **your** skills when working as part of a group.

Successful groups:

- plan well
- make sure there are clearly defined roles for every member of the group
- review regularly and carefully
- do not allow one individual to dominate
- remember the assessment criteria, and that while 'working successfully as a group' is something that can be rewarded, it is each person's individual planning and research, etc. that is being assessed in the end
- are very careful in their record-keeping so there is strong evidence of **individual** contributions
- remain a cohesive unit throughout the process.

Less successful groups:

- lack evidence of individual contributions
- allow one individual to dominate: it can become a vehicle for one person's ego
- disintegrate because of the lack of commitment on the part of one or more of the group
- do not keep good records.

Working in a group

Groups can produce excellent projects, provided **individual** members of the group remember the assessment criteria.

Record-keeping

Learning goals

By the end of the chapter you should be able to:

■ Show how vital it is for the success of your project to keep detailed and accurate records
■ Use relevant records to evidence your work
■ Appreciate the importance of keeping backups or copies of your work.

In the formal OCR specifications for the Extended Project, each of the sections covering the assessment criteria (how marks are allocated), begins with the phrase, 'The student will provide evidence of...'. You need to provide accurate, legible and relevant records as evidence of your planning and research; this is an essential skill to learn.

In the age of the computer, digital camera and mobile phone, record-keeping has become much easier. If you are depending on digital records however, always make sure that your material is backed up.

KEEPING RECORDS

✓ Good record-keeping by you is vital for success in the Extended Project.

In addition to the project itself (regardless of its format), two documents need to be sent to OCR for external moderation. Both are downloadable from the OCR site:

1 The VTT or Verification of Topic and Title. Getting this ready is the responsibility of the supervisor and it is intended to ensure that your supervisor asks you the right questions when you are starting out and keeps you on the right course. It is worthwhile looking at this document as it gives a good picture of what the role of your supervisor is, and how much help you can receive without affecting your marks. You can find the VTT at http://www.ocr.org.uk/qualifications/ projects/extended_project/documents.html.

PUTTING INTO PRACTICE

In previous projects, the most successful supervisor/student relationships have tended to arise when the supervisor was not an expert on the chosen project. Supervision inevitably had a focus on the skills such as planning and resourcing, for which the student gained marks. There were occasionally problems when the supervisor knew a great deal about the chosen topic, and tried to direct operations too much; this led to poor AO1 and AO2 marks. ● ● ●

2 The PPR or Pupil Progression Record. This is your responsibility and it is vital that you take it very seriously. Download your own copy from the OCR site and keep it carefully.

You can find a copy of the PPR at http://www.ocr.org.uk/qualifications/projects/extended_project/documents.html.

In addition, it is critical that you keep thorough, accurate and detailed records of all that you do, from the day you first start to think about the broad topic of your project, right through to the day of completion.

You need to think carefully about how you keep records (always backing up digital files). You also need to think very carefully about what records you need to keep. This should form a vital part of the planning process: the simple rule is, if in doubt, keep everything and then back it up.

A student doing a dissertation on 'Gordon Brown as Chancellor of the Exchequer – disaster or saviour?' might need recorded evidence of:

- The briefing and teaching given for the Extended Project.
- When and why the student came up with the idea.
- The range of skills taught for the EP and what the student had learned from them.
- How the student went from the broad idea of being interested in politics/economics and Gordon Brown MP to the actual title.
- The decision-making on the type of format: why a dissertation rather than a report/investigation?
- The timeline for the whole project, showing what problems the student might face.
- Thinking about the skills to be used or learned to complete the project, for example, financial analysis, use of mathematical models, interview skills, managing data, or explaining statistics.

- Evaluation of the various resources used, perhaps interviews with different types of people such as academics, politicians and businesspeople, various media, academic studies, Brown's speeches and writings, etc. This is vital for the AO2 and AO4 marks.
- Evaluation of the research done, with clear evidence of the 'wide' range of resources used.
- Recording changes in title/format/approach and reasons for this.
- Recording progress, or lack of it, and the reasons for this.
- Regular reviews. What is working? What is not? Why? What would I do better next time? What advice would I give to another student?
- The presentation (or film) and review of that process.

These records would be in addition to the 5,000 word dissertation.

A student making an artefact for their project, for example 'A miniature working model of George Stephenson's Rocket', would follow largely the same record-keeping approach as the dissertation writer, but would need to focus more on recording the following:

EVIDENCE
Remember that the key is to provide evidence to those who are marking your work in your school or college. The external moderator may also wish to look at your work and evidence, to check that your school/college is marking at the same standard as everyone else and is not being too harsh or generous.

- some of the advanced skills needed to complete the project, e.g. metallurgy/welding
- the range of skills, from historical research to practical experimentation
- the problems which arose and how they were (hopefully) solved
- visual/photographic evidence.

EVIDENCE
Remember, no evidence, no marks.

It is also vital if you are working in a group that you take enormous care to record carefully your contribution both within the group and to the group's work as a whole. You need to ensure that somebody else does not collect the marks which are rightfully yours; careful planning and proper record-keeping will avoid this.

Presentation

Learning goals

By the end of the chapter you should be able to:

- Prepare for a presentation
- Appreciate the range of methods which can be used to 'present' your work
- Select a suitable presentation method for your project
- Understand the importance of your presentation to your final marks.

Although there is no absolute requirement to do a formal presentation, some form of public presentation is an excellent idea. Remember that for A04 there is a requirement to:

'Provide evidence that a sophisticated and wide range of communication skills and media have been used to present a perceptive, effective and comprehensive review of the development and outcome of the project.'

And

'The presentation has met and exceeded the needs of its intended specialist and/or non-specialist audience.'

You should see the presentation not only as an opportunity to acquire new skills, but as a vital opportunity to demonstrate the range of skills you have acquired during the course of the project.

You should design your presentation with the need to focus on displaying those skills in mind, rather than extensive content. For example:

1 This is how I thought of the broad idea, translated the idea into a workable project, and planned and managed the whole project from beginning to end **mostly on my own**.
   (a) This is the **wide range** of resources I used (comment on the value of those different resources and on the skills you used to obtain those resources).
   (b) These are the **skills/technologies** I used to make the project work (such as problem-solving, decision-taking, etc.).
   (c) This is my **evaluation** of the whole project and my work on it.

You should encourage critical questions to which your answers demonstrate clearly how well you have:

- planned
- researched
- developed
- realised
- evaluated your project.

Modest presentation and gentle questioning will fail to bring out the strengths of the project and your achievement in learning new skills. Make sure the presentation has the right focus. If it is part of a group project, make sure your contribution is absolutely clear and can be assessed.

HOW TO SUCCEED

Make the presentation work to your advantage.

Choosing a presentation format

The range of possible presentation formats is huge, and will depend to a certain extent on the number of students in your school/college doing the project and also on the nature of the project itself. What might be right for a group project setting up a small business may not be right for someone who has written a play.

Work with your supervisor on this issue, trying hard to ensure that whatever format the presentation takes, it enables you to demonstrate and be assessed on the key skills.

Possible presentation formats might be:

- Standing up in front of a small or large group, which must include those who are assessing you, as well as some specialist and/or non-specialist audience (remember, you must be able to communicate to both).You do not have to present PowerPoint slides, but they can be useful evidence that you have done an appropriate presentation.
- Showing your play/production to a group of fellow students and assessors, followed by a 'question and answer' session.
- Having your report analysed by an intended audience (e.g. a report on local youth services by local councillors) and being questioned on it.
- Being questioned on your local business plan by the local Chamber of Commerce.

In previous projects, some colleges worked on the 'Open Evening' plan where each student/group had a stand and was questioned by staff, governors, students and parents, some of whom had been briefed to question appropriately.

KEEPING RECORDS

✓ Always ensure that all aspects of the presentation are properly recorded by the appropriate means.

Presentation skills

Remember that making a presentation is a critical opportunity to demonstrate skills and have those skills properly assessed. You should welcome positive and even forceful questioning; this is ideal preparation for university and job interviews.

Remember that you are the expert (if you have prepared properly), and plan your presentation carefully with those assessment criteria in mind. How can the presentation demonstrate:

- your planning skills?
- your impressive research?
- that you can actually achieve something, and present it on your own?
- what you have learned from doing the project, which you can apply in employment or further education?

Assessment objectives and criteria

Learning goals

By the end of the chapter you should be able to:

- Identify the work needed to address each assessment outcome
- Appreciate the allocation of marks for each section of your project.

How your project will be assessed is vital to your understanding of what the project involves. You need to know what marks are awarded for, and why. Your school or college will do the initial marking, which will then be moderated by OCR or your awarding body. Some projects will always be selected by exam boards to ensure that the centre is not marking more harshly or leniently than other centres.

If the exam board feels that your centre is marking too stringently throughout, the board will adjust all the marks upwards; the same applies if the exam board feels the centre is being generous, in which case the marks will be adjusted downwards. However, if the exam board feels that the marking is inconsistent or very different from what it should be, then it will re-mark the whole centre. If a student is unhappy about their result, they have a right of appeal to the exam board, who will re-mark the project.

When your school/college teachers sit down to mark your project, they have very clear guidelines on this process, which can be seen on the OCR website. It is well worth downloading those marking guidelines and putting them in the front of your file to remind yourself how to achieve top marks.

There are four broad **assessment objectives** for which your school/college's internal examiners can give marks. They are outlined in Table 3, and explored fully in Assessment Objectives 1-4.

Moderator's hint
Remind yourself regularly of the assessment criteria.

Assessment Objective number	Description of Assessment Objective	Percentage of overall mark
Assessment Objective 1	Managing a project	20%
Assessment Objective 2	Using resources	20%
Assessment Objective 3	Developing and realising a project	40%
Assessment Objective 4	Reviewing the project	20%

Table 3 The Assessment Objective Criteria

HOW TO SUCCEED

Remember, marks are given only for the skills listed above, nothing else.

Assessment Objective 1: Managing a project

Learning goals

By the end of the chapter you should be able to:

- Manage a project from start to finish
- Identify the main stages of project management
- Use planning tools to help manage your project
- Organise your filing system to help manage the project.

The OCR specification

Assessment Objective 1 is allocated 20 per cent of the total marks.

The first part of each point below is taken straight from the OCR specification, the rules which govern the Extended Project. The examiners will be looking at this document when they are allocating marks to your work. If you meet those objectives in full then you are entitled to full marks. The text in brackets afterwards explains the different points more fully.

To get full marks for this AO, the student [you] will have to provide good evidence that you have, with little or no help from teachers/others:

Determined a suitable topic and produced a piece of work that reflects a design proposed to and endorsed by, their teacher/mentor.

(You had the initial idea; you developed the idea and created a feasible topic; you then received the support of your supervisor for it.)

Taken full and personal responsibility for the whole project, planning and managing every aspect of it.

(You did it all. You resisted all spoon-feeding, and you demonstrated what you can do. You carried out all the planning and managing. You anticipated problems and showed evidence of contingency planning. If things went wrong, you did not blame someone else, but analysed why it went wrong and worked out how you would ensure this would not happen again.)

If you were working as part of a group, then you would have taken responsibility for identifiable parts of the group's project, directing and monitoring aspects of the work of the group and clearly taking leadership for identifiable aspects of group decision-making.

(If you are part of a group, you need to make sure that your part is easy to spot. Note the part about 'directing and monitoring'; keeping evidence of everything that you have done is vital here.)

Clearly developed a sophisticated range of organisational, IT, decision-making and problem-solving skills, and used them creatively to realise the project, and effectively managing changing circumstances.

(Keep the focus on the skills more than the content and don't worry if things change. The skills that will gain the high marks are your ability to organise yourself and your work, to make decisions, and solve problems.)

Completing the project within the agreed time schedule and meeting most of the intermediate goals.

(Finish it on time and make sure your objectives were met.)

EVIDENCE

Remember to provide evidence that you have done the planning and organising.

To achieve full marks (20 per cent of the total) for this assessment objective, you need to do the following:

- Have firm evidence that **you** had the initial idea and then carried it through the various stages to final completion, with only minimal support from tutors and others.
- Plan it very thoroughly, but be flexible when necessary.
- Prove, if you were part of a group, that **you** contributed **substantially** to the initial concept or idea, and to all the stages through to completion.
- Keep to the agreed timetable and allow your supervisors/assessors time to assess it properly before their submission to the exam board.

However, you will not be successful if you:

- were told what to do for your project
- were told how to do it
- had to be nagged endlessly to do it
- did not complete it on time

Your supervisor and the exam board will want to see the following evidence to prove that you have met this assessment objective:

- A supervisor-endorsed record and/or diary to show how the project was decided on, developed and actually carried out. You must take responsibility for ensuring that this happens.

- The amount of guidance and direction which was given to you by others must be absolutely clear (resist all attempts to spoon-feed!). Keep a careful record of all of this.
- This record must also very clearly identify what skills were developed and used by you, and the level of proficiency attained.
- Your school or college may suggest a timetable for you; make absolutely sure that you then personalise it to fit your project.

You can see why keeping a very detailed record of everything is critical. OCR will want to see that evidence, and if you feel you have been under-marked by your teacher and appeal to OCR, then you have to produce that evidence. Without evidence there can be neither marks nor appeal.

Planning the Extended Project

Successful projects don't just happen. It would be an interesting world if they did. Everything we do requires some kind of planning or forethought. Imagine going shopping without taking any money or credit card to pay for your intended purchases; it would be a complete failure.

If you have to travel two miles to get to college for 9 a.m., what time do you set off? This depends on whether you walk, cycle, drive, receive a lift, use a bus or train. Each of these options requires separate consideration (or planning) due to the different nature of each mode of transport, and the knock-on effect of traffic building up at 9 a.m.

The reflective learner

If you are taking the Extended Project as part of a Diploma, you will have heard about the reflective learner. This is not a new concept to most people, but the 'new' approach within the Diploma is that planning and reflective practices are documented or evidenced in other ways, whereas previously, they just 'happened'.

Everything we do causes a result. We analyse the result, decide whether we liked the result, consider how it could be done differently: better, quicker, cheaper, more enjoyably, etc. Most of the time, we do this without thinking about calling it reflective practice.

How might this apply to the example of getting to college, given above? Assume you cycle to college: every day you can make the journey in about 10 minutes, except on Wednesdays because it is market day, and as there is much more traffic on the roads, your journey takes longer and you are late. You might reflect on the following alternative actions:

- Is there another route?
- Is there a bus you could use, which might mean setting off earlier?
- Could you walk?
- Could you leave your cycle at a friend's house, halfway to college?

There are several possible alternative decisions and methods which could be used, even including getting up earlier and setting off on your bike 10 minutes earlier.

This simple example illustrates that reflective practices are part of everything we do. Reflection on any activity can then be followed by a 'plan' of what to do. This is put into place, we carry out the plan, then analyse the outcomes. We might even think of some other change to make the outcome even more acceptable.

Carrying out your Extended Project requires these actions, and the only difference is that you need to evidence it all – write it down, keep a log or diary, take photos, etc.

How do we plan?

Let's look further at how we plan things. We all like to eat, but a good meal doesn't just happen, either. If you are going to make a meal, you need to do some serious planning first. A major culinary feast (and feat) is to prepare a traditional Sunday roast dinner.

Make a list of the typical contents of such a meal (or any other meal which you prefer).

Your list could include the following:

- potatoes
- carrots
- cabbage
- broccoli
- parsnips
- gravy
- meat
- Yorkshire puddings.

You want to eat at 1 p.m. Consider the following questions:

- What time do you start preparing the meal?
- What do you do first?
- How many pans do you need? (How many do you have?)
- How many cooker rings are needed?
- How many people are you feeding?
- What could go wrong?

Imagine that your Extended Project is to plan and prepare a Sunday roast (such a project would definitely prepare you for the future, but you wouldn't want it to take 120 hours).

Your teacher/supervisor may be a person who specialises in eating such a meal, but may not be able to advise you about the subject of preparing it.

This would be a perfect scenario, because your supervisor's role would be to support you with your project management skills, not with cooking a meal. Your supervisor could provide advice about planning and analysing the work, evaluating and suggesting sources of reference if you get stuck, and with all other planning and management skills required to complete a meal without telling you how to prepare and cook it. That's your job.

The need for research

So how do you find out the answers to the above questions? You could ask or consult:

- a friend
- a parent
- a grandparent
- a chef
- a lecturer in catering
- a restaurateur
- a food technologist
- Wikipedia.

Write down what they tell you or keep records of your findings. This is research at a practical level, and you may need to refer to it later, hence the need to record it all.

You could carry out further research on the Internet, and looking up cookery books and recipes might be helpful as well.

Once you have all this information, what other considerations are there? What could go wrong?

- Food poisoning?
- Something not cooked for long enough?
- Dishes or trays placed too high or too low in the oven?
- Oven temperature too high or too low?
- You like vegetables 'al dente' and your reference source suggests they should be soft.

If someone becomes ill after eating the food, or even if there is part of the meal which you don't like, what sort of things would you need to evaluate, reflect on, manage, improve, etc., to ensure that this doesn't happen next time?

Making use of your reference notes

The first logical step is to check your research notes to locate the source of the information which caused the problem, so keep good, effective notes. Perhaps a new recipe book suggested that carrots should not be pealed, and then everyone thought they tasted earthy, or perhaps the meat is raw and pink in the middle, and you don't like the taste.

What could be reviewed and changed for next time? Perhaps the eggs you used were large, whereas the person who told you to use three eggs in the Yorkshire pudding mix only used small eggs; or the flour was different; or you used skimmed milk and they meant full-fat, etc.

Without notes to refer back to, it is very difficult and time-consuming to find a solution after you have reflected on the product. Nobody expects to find accurate Harvard referencing within a recipe for a Sunday roast (unless this is the topic of your Extended Project), but keep a record of where the details for your recipe came from, to allow you to find them and congratulate them for the fantastic meal (or perhaps a forensic pathologist would like to know who gave you the recipe which poisoned you or one of your guests).

Planning skills

Having evaluated the need for planning, let's take a look at what kind of planning might be needed for the Extended Project. Once you've found the subject for your project:

- You need to decide what's important and what can be skipped.
- Make a note of your ideas and filter through them.
- Your teacher will be able to help by teaching you how to plan a project.
- Prepare an outline plan for your work.
- You have approximately 120 guided learning hours (GLH); you will need all of these and probably more, as the Extended Project is a large piece of work.
- Putting the evidence together takes time – allow for this.
- Although it seems a long way off at present, doing the evaluation takes longer than you may imagine, so evaluate each part as you go along, and then evaluate everything you have done. Say what you would do differently if you were to do it again. Kolb's cycle of plan, do, reflect, review, can help you. This is something which we all do all the time, but it needs documenting and evidencing. Make an evaluation plan – evaluate all the time.
- Keep evidence. Don't throw anything away until the project is all finished and marked.

Different outcomes to the Extended Project

You may wish to:

- design or redesign a product, process or system
- make a product or artefact or a model of something
- perform – a song, dance or recital
- write a report or produce a dissertation about a topic which interests you
- carry out an in-depth investigation, for a variety of reasons.

All of these are possible, and you can even combine two or more of these, in agreement with your supervisor and depending on the topic which you select.

You can even change your mind, but the advice here is to document and evidence your thoughts and the reasons for changing your mind. Projects and design ideas are changed in real life, at the start, in the middle, near the end (although that is difficult to do), so changing your mind will not be frowned upon. You need to keep evidence to show why you changed your mind; this demonstrates problem-solving skills, which is a difficult area to cover, but it may happen naturally if you changed your mind. Changing your mind or project type may be congratulated, indicating that your project management skills allowed you to recognise that something needed changing or revisiting, and you planned it – then did it.

Your outcome may not be the one you intended to achieve. This doesn't matter. The content or subject is totally irrelevant to the marks you will be awarded. Obviously, it helps if the content is good, interesting and thorough, but this qualification is about project management, not the subject content.

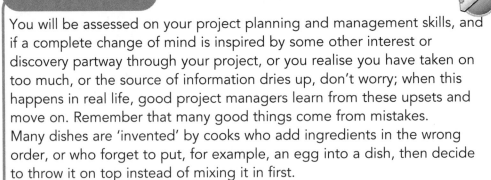

HOW TO SUCCEED

You will be assessed on your project planning and management skills, and if a complete change of mind is inspired by some other interest or discovery partway through your project, or you realise you have taken on too much, or the source of information dries up, don't worry; when this happens in real life, good project managers learn from these upsets and move on. Remember that many good things come from mistakes.

Many dishes are 'invented' by cooks who add ingredients in the wrong order, or who forget to put, for example, an egg into a dish, then decide to throw it on top instead of mixing it in first.

KEEPING RECORDS

To succeed, you should:
- ✓ record and document such actions
- ✓ include a review of the reasons for or causes of the changes
- ✓ write down your ideas and thoughts
- ✓ make notes about any diversions
- ✓ clearly lay out any new plans, or preferably amendments, to the original plan.

Real plans need to be changed and you need to evidence the 'actual' timings against the 'planned' timings. This will show how you managed the progress of the project and, more importantly, how you solved ongoing problems, which prepares you well for life and employment in the future.

Moderator's hint

If a candidate's project follows their initial plan exactly, it usually suggests that the plan was not done until the project was finished. You may think that retrospective planning will make your planning look good. However, an experienced teacher, assessor or moderator who checks your assessor/supervisor's work to agree your final score, will spot this immediately.

If you select to write a dissertation, you should aim for 5,000 words. This sounds long, but if the project is of real interest to you, 5,000 words is not much at all. What if you only write 4,921 words, or even 3,984 words? Or what if the dissertation runs into 6,000 or almost 7,000 words? A moderator will not mark down a good project if it is over or under the word count. A moderator will only mark down a project if it does not address the assessment outcomes. Good project report management skills should include 'minimisation' of adjectives and the removal of repeated sections.

Moderator's hint

When a moderator at the exam board checks your work and your teacher's assessment score, it may be moderated upwards, or your score may go down. To avoid this, include as much relevant evidence as you can, without excess padding.

PUTTING INTO PRACTICE

In the future, you may need to submit some written work to be published, either in a technical or professional journal, or in a newspaper or a magazine. If you exceed the word limit, the editor will do the 'trimming' to achieve the correct word count. Wouldn't you rather trim it to ensure the main thrust of your work is seen by all readers? See this project as practice for future writing. ● ● ●

Using IT in planning

Using IT (and making mistakes) teaches us many things. Every time you sit down to write your project, say on a word processor, save the file with that day's date in the title,

Moderator's hint

Ask someone to read your work and tell them to be ruthless with their suggested clippings. Read it alongside the mark bands (like your assessor and moderator will do). Material which does not clearly address any of the contents of the mark band will earn zero marks, so take it out (but don't delete it yet; you might just need to put it back).

then all your old material is saved until you can confidently delete it (perhaps after you have been awarded a certificate for completing the qualification and you are happy with the grade). For example, files could be dated in the following way:

- 15th May 2010
- 22nd May 2010
- 4th June 2010
- 17th June 2010.

However, when you try to open one of them, they appear in alpha-numeric order:

- 4th June 2010
- 15th May 2010
- 17th June 2010
- 22nd May 2010.

Or even:

- 15th May 2010
- 17th June 2010
- 22nd May 2010
- 4th June 2010.

This makes it difficult to find the most recent file; you could then spend three hours adding material to an out-of-date version of your work. Instead, try using the following system to date your files:

- 2010 05 15
- 2010 05 22
- 2010 06 04
- 2010 06 17.

The files will appear in chronological order, up or down depending on how your files are set up. You can put your own personal file name or title after the date numbers, to help you pick it out from all the other files which you may have saved on that date.

Hitting the word count

If you are summarising some research, but cannot do so in, for example, less than 2,000 words, refer to it with little more than a passing comment in your report, and put your main summary in the back of the report as an appendix.

Appendices are not part of the main body, so the words are not counted towards the overall total. However, don't forget to refer the reader to it from the main body of the text, or it will be ignored and your project management/reporting skills will not be scored very highly.

Remember, though, that appendices should **not** be used just to bulk out the work; you should include items which have helped you put your work together. Also remember not to place important material into an appendix without referring to it with a brief overview in your report. Appendices are not looked at unless referred to in the main report, so if you don't refer to it, leave it out.

Moderator's hint
The plan and other 'project management' material are very important parts of the project – do **not** put them in the appendix.

HOW TO SUCCEED

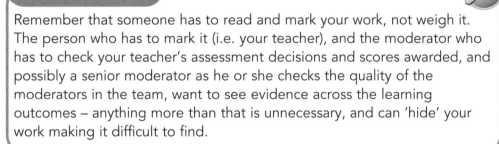

Remember that someone has to read and mark your work, not weigh it. The person who has to mark it (i.e. your teacher), and the moderator who has to check your teacher's assessment decisions and scores awarded, and possibly a senior moderator as he or she checks the quality of the moderators in the team, want to see evidence across the learning outcomes – anything more than that is unnecessary, and can 'hide' your work making it difficult to find.

If you have to move material to the appendix to reduce your overall word count, try trimming and summarising the subject material; place it in the appendix, with a summary in the main body which refers readers to the appendix.

Writing for a practical project

Do practical projects (making something) reduce the amount of written work? Some students dislike writing so choose to make something for their Extended Project. However, don't make the mistake of thinking that writing is only required for the report or dissertation.

All types of outcome must include a written part, along with your PPR (Project Progression Record). The requirement is for between 1,000 and 1,500 words alongside the artefact or product. This text should provide background information, introduction, analysis of your work and actions, what went wrong, what went well, your review, etc.

Organisational skills

You've probably been told many times by different teachers that you need to improve your organisational skills. You certainly need to have good organisational skills to manage an effective project. You also need personal drive – an enthusiasm to keep yourself going.

As part of your planning, you need to set targets and follow your overall plan by completing work in short episodic bursts, especially the bits you find less interesting or exciting.

Moderator's hint
If your chosen extended project idea doesn't fill you with enthusiasm, then pick another project topic.

Set yourself some reasonable and realistic deadlines, and stick to them. You could even try to finish some of them earlier than planned; if so, document this, and say why you finished earlier than expected. Was it good work on your part? Was it just poor planning and inaccurately estimating the duration? Did it provide you with spare time to complete another section, making it even better than planned?

Try not to leave your Extended Project log for a week or two because you are getting too interested in the work: update it every time you do some more work. If you miss a week, you'll forget to do it and forget what you have done, then it becomes a chore and may become the weakness in your project.

EVIDENCE
Keep your project log book up to date — use it like a personal planner. If you have an electronic gadget which you can use for this, this can be even more effective. Keep a back-up of all your work on a regular basis, or you will be faced with starting again if some data gets lost.

- Record and evaluate everything you do.
- Discuss your records with others as you go along.
- If you decide not to do something which was on your plan, record this and say why you are not doing it.

This may all be useful evidence to include in your final project to demonstrate your project management skills. Remember: this qualification is about your project management skills, which are more important than your knowledge of your subject or topic area.

HOW TO SUCCEED

If you feel that you are running out of time, concentrate on addressing the assessment criteria, which are all written to focus on the project management skills. Marks are awarded for demonstration of these skills, not particularly for the interesting information contained within your project.

Setting the timescale for your plan

Start by thinking about when it will be (must be) completed.

- Will it be submitted in the January or June series? Check this with your teacher.
- Are you doing the Extended Project over a full academic year, or starting it, say, at Easter in year 11 to complete for Christmas in year 12?
- A January submission may allow time to resubmit if you have time (and energy), and want a better grade or a second chance.
- You may want to complete it early in order to concentrate on your other studies, be they GCE A Levels or the Advanced Diploma.

Time is a critical factor in all projects. There is never enough time. Work has been described as something which expands until it fills the time you have available to do it. To help you produce a plan which you can keep to, you need to use some planning skills.

Timelines/critical paths

Consider exactly what you need to do and break it down into small, manageable chunks.

- What do you need to achieve altogether?
- What can you achieve in the first month?
- What would you expect to be doing by halfway through the planned duration?

These all seem like reasonable questions, but if you do not have reasonable answers for them at any time during your project, you are not managing it very successfully.

Moderator's hint
Perhaps you have been seduced into thinking that your project topic is more important than managing your project ... this is wrong!

How to start planning your Extended Project

Draw a straight line across a sheet of paper. The left-hand end of this line is the time at which you start, and the right-hand end is the time by which you will have completed your project.

Once you have broken your Extended Project down into a list of things which need to be done throughout its duration, you can start to estimate where they will fit along this timeline. This is the start of your effective planning.

EVIDENCE
If there is evidence of the activity described taking place (even if it is drawn by hand and the paper is a bit scruffy from the excessive use of an eraser), the moderator will see that you understand how to start making a plan.

Don't worry that you don't know how long it will take you to do some part or section of your project. Some parts may take a week, or perhaps they may take a month. Estimate these times: somewhere between perhaps three or four weeks. As you reach that point in time, you may be able to start early – or you may have to start late.

When you are three-quarters of the way through, you may have planned to start your final write-up, but still have much to do to complete what you are making.

In such a case, would you:

1 Try to race on and do the work quicker to make sure you covered everything to complete the artefact?
2 Start the final write-up, spending a lot of time analysing what went wrong and saying how you could improve it next time?

Moderator's hint

Remember that you are being assessed on your project management skills, not on your ability to finish a piece of work about your chosen topic within a limited time. You don't even need to finish the piece of work, but you *do* need to finish every aspect of your project management records.

See the assessment criteria (later) or ask your teacher to talk you through it again.

Read the advice in the Moderator's hint feature on the right.

Gantt charts – a simple introduction

This section will introduce you (or re-introduce you) to some well tried and tested techniques for planning and project management.

1 Put 'Gantt chart' into a search engine, such as Google, Yahoo or any other.
2 Follow a few leads.
3 Don't take the first explanation as being perfect; compare and evaluate your findings.

This simple activity has already proved that you are a researcher, an evaluator and a reflective learner. Check out the list of PLTS (personal, learning and thinking skills) and see what else you have done already. Refer to the PLTS in Assessment Objectives 3.

If you cannot find any simple examples of Gantt chart applications, try the one below, although it is not as simple as it first appears.

Task

Tea and toast

You want to make a cup of tea and a slice of buttered toast for your breakfast. What will be the final outcome? Perhaps an acceptable outcome would be: tea and warm, buttered toast, ready at the same time.

At what time do you want these two things to be ready (right-hand end of the timeline)? The timeline would have two parallel activities running along it, and it might become a bit messy.

You need to answer the following questions:

* How long does it take to boil the water? (How would you research that?)
* How long does it take to toast a slice of bread, then spread the butter? (How would you research that?)
* Do you like the butter melted, requiring it to be applied to hot toast, or do you prefer the toast to cool down so that the butter does not melt?
* Will you use a tea bag in the cup, or do you prefer to use a teapot?
* Tea bags or loose tea?
* Do you put the milk in the cup first, or after the tea?

Write a list of all the tasks, or type them into different cells down a column in a spreadsheet. Estimate how long each task will take. If you need accurate timings, try it out and time yourself. Aim to have a deadline of four or five minutes (or even less) to create your tea and toast breakfast.

* What needs to be done first?
* Can any activity or task be started late, without spoiling the final outcome?
* Using project management vocabulary 'is there a critical path?'

A critical path network (CPN) is a series of activities which cannot be delayed without causing an overall delay in the complete project. The timing of these activities is critical (the clue is in the title!).

Table 4 provides preparation for a Gantt Chart.

Making a hot cup of tea and a slice of warm buttered toast				
Activities	Activity code	Duration in seconds	Pre-requisites	Common completion times
Put water in kettle	A	10		
Boil water	B	120	A	
Rinse out tea pot	C	5		
Warm tea pot	D	30	C	
Put tea in tea pot	E	10	D	
Pour boiling water into tea pot	F	5	B, E	
Remove cup from cabinet	G	10		
Remove milk from fridge	H	5		
Allow tea to brew	I	180	F	
Put milk in cup	J	5	G, H	
Pour tea into cup	K	5	I, J	
Add sugar	L	5	K	
Stir tea in the cup	M	5	L	end with S
Put bread in toaster	N	10		
Toaster operating	O	150	N	
Remove toast	P	10	O	
Remove butter from fridge	Q	5		
Apply butter to toast	R	10	P, Q	
Cut toast and put on plate	S	5	R	end with M

Table 4 Preparation for a Gantt Chart

From Table 4, it can be seen that two activities need to be completed at the same time. Hence, start at the end of the plan and work towards the start of the plan. This is usual because we are working towards an outcome, a cup of tea and warm toast.

There is another step to this – see Table 5. Rearrange the activities, which can be cut and pasted in a spreadsheet. Because we don't know the duration yet, starting at the right-hand side of a page could lead to you running out of room at the left-hand side. Hence, a spreadsheet which grows down the page makes it helpful to start with the end at the top. The height of each cell can represent 5 seconds (the smallest increment for any activity).

Completed							
Pre-requisite	Activities	Code	Duration	Pre-requisite	Activity	Code	Duration
L	Stir tea in the cup	M	5	R	Cut toast and put on plate	S	5
K	Add sugar	L	5	P, Q	Apply butter to toast	R	10
I, J	Pour tea into cup	K	5		Remove butter from fridge	Q	5
G, H	Put milk in cup	J	5	O	Remove toast	P	10
	Remove milk from fridge	H	5	N	Toaster operating	O	150
	Remove cup from cabinet	G	10		Put bread in toaster	N	10
F	Allow tea to brew	I	180				
B, E	Pour boiling water into tea pot	F	5s				
D	Put tea in tea pot	E	10s				
C	Warm tea pot	D	30s				
	Rinse out tea pot	C	5s				
A	Boil water	B	120s				
	Put water in kettle	A	10s				

Table 5 Completed activities

Notice that each activity has a name, reference letter, duration and pre-requisites, where appropriate. This gives us some idea of the order of things.

Moderator's hint

Producing the plan might not be easy, and it may be more or less complicated than this one. It doesn't matter: what does matter is that you include a plan at the start of your project (not in an appendix).

Now for the Gantt chart: see Figure 1. It soon becomes obvious that a simple task of making a tea and toast breakfast can become very complicated, when all we were trying to do was to plan it out to ensure a good result. Imagine anyone having to make breakfast AND a roast Sunday dinner on one day. This makes for a very busy day!

This should show you that creating a plan for your project will not be easy, but it will help to move it nearer to being a good result.

Other planning methods

You could also use a PERT (Project [or Programme] Evaluation and Review Technique).

If you research the meaning of PERT, you will soon encounter CPN. Critical path networks allow you to see which tasks in a project **must** be completed on time or the whole project is delayed and incomplete.

The specific tasks which fall within the critical path are critical to the success of the project, hence the name. Research and reporting on the use of PERT or CPN would make a good project in itself.

Before any of these tools can be used, you must list the individual tasks or activities which you will carry out between starting and finishing your project. Hence, you need to identify the steps required to arrive, from your initial idea and project focus, at the finished product, dissertation or report, or performance.

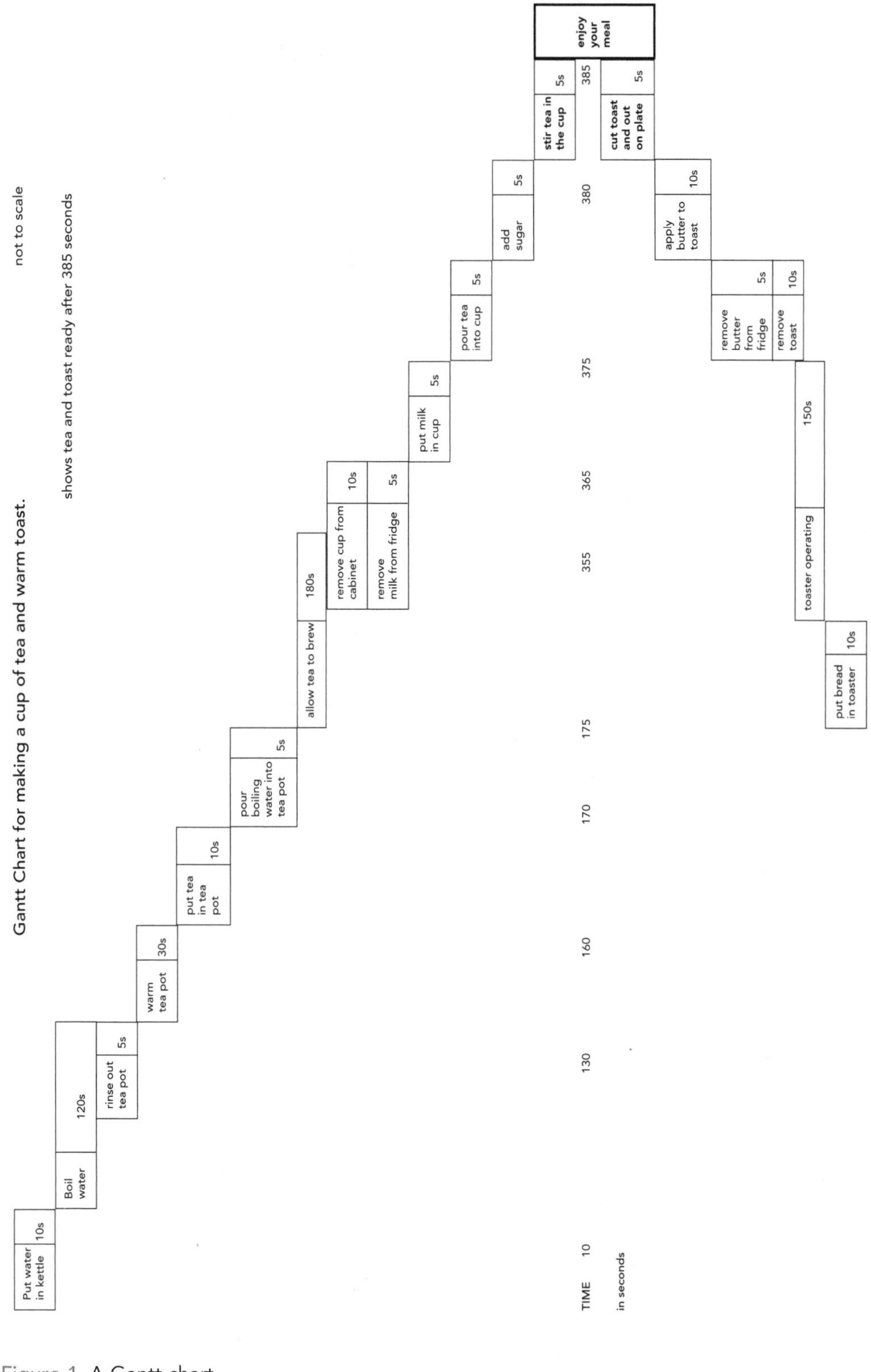

Gantt Chart for making a cup of tea and warm toast.

not to scale

shows tea and toast ready after 385 seconds

Put water in kettle	10s

Boil water — 120s

rinse out tea pot — 5s

warm tea pot — 30s

put tea in tea pot — 10s

pour boiling water into tea pot — 5s

allow tea to brew — 180s

remove cup from cabinet — 10s

remove milk from fridge — 5s

put milk in cup — 5s

pour tea into cup — 5s

add sugar — 5s

stir tea in the cup — 5s

enjoy your meal

cut toast and out on plate — 5s

apply butter to toast — 10s

remove butter from fridge — 5s

remove toast — 10s

toaster operating — 150s

put bread in toaster — 10s

TIME — 10 — 130 — 160 — 170 — 175 — 355 — 365 — 375 — 380 — 385

in seconds

Figure 1 A Gantt chart

47

Assessment Objective 2: Using resources

Learning goals

By the end of the chapter you should be able to:

- Make full use of your project supervisor
- Select other people to use as advisers
- Carry out your own research
- Make effective use of your collected data
- Avoid losing all your marks, by not cheating.

The OCR specification

Assessment Objective 2 is allocated 20 per cent of the marks.

The first part of each point below is taken straight from the OCR specification, the rules which govern the Extended Project. They describe what the student will need to provide as evidence for this part of the project. The examiners will be looking at this document when they are allocating marks to your work. If you meet those objectives in full then you are entitled to full marks. The text in brackets afterwards explains the different points more fully.

The student will provide evidence that:

They used a wide range of resources to obtain, select, collate and analyse data suitable to the project. Little or no guidance was given on the choice or interpretation of the sources by the supervisor.

(You researched widely. You used lots of different **types** of resources and demonstrated lots of initiative in looking for those resources. You then sensibly selected a reasonable amount of information to use for your project and analysed it carefully. You did not receive much help from your supervisor for this work.)

A sophisticated and perceptive understanding of the connections and linkages between different types of resource and the complexities inherent in the project has been developed.

Moderator's hint
Note that the specification refers to your 'supervisor'. You can also seek advice/views from other people or specialists, but you must keep a critical record of it.

(You showed you were well aware of the possible links between different types of resource, such as the oral and the visual, and understood any complex issues which arose as the project developed.)

Moderator's hint
Always note carefully the value to your project of the resources used.

A wide range of the appropriate technology and related technical skills have been used to aid the collection of information and data. E-learning has been used skilfully and critically to further the aims of the project, where appropriate.

(Don't just download from the Internet; really develop those research skills. You need to demonstrate that you have been creative and independent in your research.)

Where relevant, a wide range of appropriate information and/or data has been obtained working with others in the context of engagement in a business, social-community venture/enterprise or through involvement in a local, regional or international team Extended Project. The learner has offered leadership or direction in this context.

(If you are part of a group project, keep the evidence **of your own work** and ensure that you are not just a passenger. For the top marks you have to show leadership of the group in some aspects of the group's work.)

It is vital that you bear these assessment criteria in mind when you are doing your research, so you will receive a straight zero for the criteria if you:

- only chat casually to a few people as research,
- read only a few local newspaper articles,
- don't grasp the links between what you are told and what you read,
- use none of the obvious technical tools to assist your research,
- sit back and relax on a group project, letting the others do the work and talking.

HOW TO SUCCEED

It is the **wide** range of resources used that is vital.

To get the A* you need to do the following:

- Make sure you use a wide range of different types of resources which are important to the project. Demonstrate that you have **thought carefully** about the value of those resources and not just felt, 'Oh well, it was in Wikipedia/the newspaper so it must be OK'.

- Grasp the links/connections between the resources used.
- Use the relevant technology (but not just for the sake of it. If totally inappropriate, the marks can be allocated elsewhere in AO2).

The evidence you will need to produce at the end for this must be a **full** record of those sources used. Keep a personal and accurate record, and remember to comment on the value of each resource to you. Make sure also that your supervisor is aware of whatever new skills you have learned, as that will gain you marks. If you are part of a group, make absolutely sure that your supervisor is fully aware of **your** involvement in all aspects of the project.

What are assessors looking for?

The key words for those who are marking the 'research' part of your project are 'plan, carry out, independence'. Your assessors will be looking for very clear evidence that you have completed the following tasks:

Plan your research very carefully
Show that you thought through what information you needed to find and where you would find it, before you embarked on the project. For example, if you were doing a project on the use of surgery for cosmetic defects, show that you could actually access the views of those people who performed or received this type of surgery.

Use a wide range of resources
If you were making a documentary film, you did not just look at other documentary films, but you might have read specialist books on documentary, making, interviewed documentary film-makers, consulted their critics, etc.

Use an appropriate range of sources of information
If you were doing a project on the media's portrayal of the NHS, then you viewed the issue from the point of view of different types of patients, as well as those who worked in the NHS at different levels.

Moderator's hint
You need to think about these resources implications while planning your project, not halfway through it.

Select the right sort of methods for collecting the information
The method of collecting information should be appropriate to the task; for example, a questionnaire on how the public view the future of public transport in a town.

Collate information from a range of resources
Make sure that your project did not depend on just a single type of resource, for example Wikipedia!

Evaluate resources very carefully

Was the resource suitable? Was it any good? Why, or why not? Always provide evidence of this. For example, in a project on the impact of recent terrorist attacks on civil liberties, show that you are aware that a victim of an attack might feel differently towards new restrictive laws on civil liberties than someone who had suffered detention without trial and was later proved to be totally innocent.

Follow up new lines of research

New areas for research might arise in the course of the project. For example, when interviewing an expert on climate change, she suggests an area to investigate which had not occurred to you before, which is more accessible and lends itself better to your project.

Consider issues like cost and availability of resources

These need to be very evident in your initial plan. Can you afford it? What happens if none of the marketing managers of local firms can see you when you are available?

Anticipate possible problems

What could go wrong? Might your boat sink? What if you break your leg and cannot coach that team?

Moderator's hint
You need to learn how to plan research as well as carry it out.

When you set out on your research, always remember to do the following:

- Plan it in detail.
- Use a wide range of different but relevant sources.
- Evaluate the research you do as you do your work; don't leave it until the end of the project.
- Record and store the results of your research carefully.
- Think about availability and access to resources before you start.
- Consider the possible cost of your research.
- Don't place too much reliance on a single source.
- Check whether you have the skills needed to use those resources.

Planning your research

It is essential to draw up a timetable for your research at a very early stage, and to discuss it with your supervisor. The timetable should cover the whole Extended Project from the day you first started to think about a topic, through the various review stages, to final submission and presentation.

The 'research' part of your planning should include:

- what research needs to be done
- when it has to be done

- how it has to be done
- the availability of the resources you might need
- how it fits in with other work/exams/holidays
- feasibility: within timescale, budget, distance, etc.
- contingencies: you might lose precious time because of illness; it might cost more than you anticipated
- time for collation of research materials, recording research, evaluation of research
- time for writing it up/doing it, presentation, submission.

Moderator's hint
Make sure that all of these points are in your initial plan.

Some projects have gone badly wrong because of simple failures in planning; for example:

- Assuming the Design/Technology workshop in school would be open and staffed throughout the summer holidays to complete an artefact. It wasn't.
- Failure to factor in the cost of museum visits.
- Not ordering books in time. Public libraries can be excellent at sourcing books for you, but they may need time to transport them from the other end of the country.

 PUTTING INTO PRACTICE

Think very carefully about the availability of resources. One project nearly failed as it was based on the assumption that Premiership footballers would readily give long interviews to students. They didn't. ● ● ●

Planning for using a wide range of resources

Inevitably every type of project will require different forms of research, and different methods of recording, storing and accessing it. You need to think about this before you start, and thereby receive AO1 marks for planning. Remember also the requirement to use a wide range of resources. What is meant by 'wide range' depends on the type of project and format chosen.

Dissertation

A dissertation on an event such as 'The fall of the Berlin Wall, 1989' or 'Bloody Sunday, 1972' might require the following:

- primary sources: ranging from actual documents to interviews with participants
- secondary sources: written at different times, perhaps from different perspectives

- interviews with experts, perhaps with conflicting views
- analysis of different types of media coverage.

Obviously if you are writing about the Battle of Hastings in 1066, some parts of the above might prove a challenge, but less so if it was the events of 'Bloody Sunday' in 1972. It pays to think about the research implications of your project before you start.

Artefact

An artefact may require different types of resources. Taking the example of designing and making a dress, the following resources may be required:

- primary sources: such as interviewing people who currently design and make dresses or have done so in the past, looking at dresses themselves
- secondary sources: histories of dress design and manufacture
- museum visits
- specialist libraries to access photos and designs
- visits to HE institutions where they train dress designers and makers.

Moderator's hint
Your supervisor can help you with selecting a 'wide range of resources'.

Production

A production, or performance where a play was being written and directed, might require:

- theatre visits
- interviews with people who are writing/have written or directed plays
- reading plays, perhaps from different periods
- reading secondary material on playwriting/directing
- reading the works of critics
- experimental workshops
- visits to drama depts/training college.

KEEPING RECORDS

✓ Think carefully about how you are going to record and store the results of your research, so that you can access this material easily when you are writing your report/dissertation.

Investigation

An investigation for example on 'Catholic teaching on abortion' might require:

- secondary sources on the history and theology of the issue
- analysis of a range of media coverage of the issue, including the Catholic press

- interviews/surveys looking at differing views from both within and outside the Roman Catholic Church
- survey of actual methods of teaching the issue
- attitudes in other counties/churches on the issue, via primary and secondary sources.

All of the above were based on actual and successful projects, so when you are thinking of a topic it is vital that you bear in mind that you need to be able to demonstrate both the importance and the necessity of at least four different types of resource. Examiners will be aware that some Extended Projects will have great challenges with resources, while others are more straightforward.

HOW TO SUCCEED

Overcoming challenges in finding resources will gain marks.

The selection of resources

Some projects may have such limited resources available that selection is not an issue (but might perhaps give pause for thought about your choice of topic?). However, with many projects the problem is not too few possible resources for research, but too many. These two points provide the key to success:

- Select a reasonable range of each type of resource. Your supervisor can help you decide what is 'reasonable'.
- Select a reasonable range within each type of resource.

So for example if you were doing an investigation into 'The influence of the media on the General Election of 2005', a suitable **range** of resources might be:

- two or three of the published 'academic' studies on the General Election
- two or three published academic studies on general media influence on politics and voting behaviour
- interviews with politicians/journalists/ordinary voters
- a study before, during, and after the election of the behaviour of:
  - the 'serious' press: one 'rightwing' and one 'leftwing'
  - the tabloid press: perhaps choose two with the largest circulations
  - local press: independent or owned by News International (Rupert Murdoch)

- radio: both national and local, commercial and BBC
- television: perhaps BBC1 and Channel Four
- the Internet.

This list certainly contains a 'wide range of resources'. No one would expect you to read every book/every newspaper on the 2005 election. If there is not a politics teacher in school to recommend academic books to read, then look it up on the Internet and search for reader reviews. Your public library should be able to order them for you; they have an excellent reservation/inter-library loan system and also access to newspaper archives, etc.

One Extended Project, which involved designing and making a piece of furniture, did not receive high marks for AO2, as the only research evident was the downloading of photos of similar pieces of furniture from the Internet, and consulting some people about what they wanted from this sort of furniture. This project was awarded a C grade. In spite of the superb effort and brilliant end product, it did not receive an A* as it was treated too much like a piece of Design and Technology coursework, and there was not the right focus on the assessment criteria.

The collation of research

Before you start your research, think carefully about how you are going to manage the resources you collect. You should devise a system of resource storage **before** you start; your school/college should give you basic training in this area. Remember also that this sort of planning ahead will gain AO1 marks.

If, for example, your project is on the work of a pioneering photographer, you may have to be able to store and then access easily the following resources:

- photographs (how? chronologically? by subject? both?)
- your notes on those photographs
- the work of contemporaries influenced by the photographer
- the technology used in taking/developing/printing
- biographical material from secondary and primary sources
- critical studies.

KEEPING RECORDS

✓ Careful planning of information storage is vital when it comes to final submission.

You need to think about the following points when planning
your resource collection:

- Why do I want it?
- How do I want to use it?
- When will I want to use it?
- What part of the project will I need it for?
- What will it provide evidence of?

Moderator's hint
Remember that this sort of advance planning will gain marks for AO1.

Different projects will have different storage/collation problems. A project
on Northumbrian folk music might need to consider how to store and
then access appropriately the following resources:

- music
- lyrics
- film of live performances
- interview notes
- notes from secondary sources
- critical reviews in the media.

By contrast, a group setting up a business might need to record, collate
and then access the following resources:

- minutes of meetings
- individual contributions to decisions and meetings
- records of individuals and groups designing, implementing, revising and
  evaluating the marketing strategy
- records of sales, costs, profits, losses, etc. (recording individual work as
  well as individual contributions to the group)
- film records of presentations
- emails
- recorded discussions.

KEEPING RECORDS

✓ Halfway through the process is too late to start to think about
record-keeping and collation: do it right from the beginning!

Evaluation and record-keeping

Remember always to evaluate (think carefully about the value of) the
resources you consider. Build in space in your record-keeping process to
do this as you work. When you write your report, you can therefore avoid
having to think 'That was a great/important resource, but I can't
remember when I saw it and why it was so valuable'. Good evaluation
gains AO4 marks and good record-keeping of your evaluation will provide

the important evidence that examiners and moderators need to see.

Record-keeping

Good record-keeping is critical to the success of your project. As always, recording will vary from project to project, but the following broad rules apply to any resource, such as data from research, notes from a book, an interview, a piece of music or a photograph:

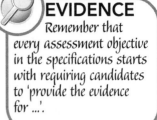

EVIDENCE
Remember that every assessment objective in the specifications starts with requiring candidates to 'provide the evidence for ...'.

- What is the important information in it which has an obvious link to my project?
- How can I access it easily again?
- How can I prove I did not just make this up?
- Is it in the right format to fit into a bibliography?
- How valuable is it?
- When was it read/viewed, etc?
- If I am asked to provide evidence for something, such as my planning, does this provide it?

Evaluation

Remember the top marks for AO4 are going for those who show 'a critical and reflective' approach to learning. Evaluation of the whole project is dealt with separately, but you need to demonstrate that you have thought carefully about the value of the resources you have used.

If you were a banker in the money-lending business, then you would always review the credit worthiness of a customer before you lent money to them. You should apply the same caution to your resources.

Moderator's hint
Words and phrases such as 'thoughtful', 'critical and reflective', 'careful analysis of information' appeared regularly in the comments on A* projects.

If you have interviewed someone as part of your research, think about:

- their level of expertise; how much do they actually know about it?
- the likelihood of bias or prejudice on their part
- whether they are saying what they actually feel or what you want to hear
- how representative they are.

Or having read a book on one part of your project, consider the following questions:

- How well was it reviewed? (check newspaper archives)
- Was it useful? How? Why?
- Was it well written?

- Was it written by an established expert, or was it a rushed job to meet popular demand?
- Why was it written?
- Why has it impressed you? If it has not, why not?

You need to bear in mind that a book by a leading Roman Catholic theologian on euthanasia will have a different slant from one by someone who has invested money in the Swiss company Dignitas, which assists voluntary suicide.

It is worth reflecting on the value and accuracy of every type of resource you use, from the photograph to the piece of music. There was once a famous photograph in a local newspaper under the heading '200 TV licence-dodgers caught'. The photograph showed only the first two people in the queue of over 200 people outside the magistrate's court. These first two people happened to be black, unlike most of the other people. What point do you think the newspaper was trying to make? Treat all evidence with initial suspicion.

Group research

Research can be a problematic area for groups, where for example:

- one person has done most of the work
- one person has done no work
- each member of the group has focused on one type of resource
- individual contributions are difficult to identify and therefore mark.

Working in a group

Identifying and marking individual contributions to group research is a common problem for the moderator.

The assessment criteria states that the **individual** student will 'use a wide range of sources ... collate ... analyse ... with little or no guidance on choice ... from teacher'.

To achieve this, ensure that each member has a clearly defined role within the group for research. The group might be working on a production with a designer, a producer, a director. Each one can then have an obvious area to plan and research. If the groups are setting up a business, then the marketing, production, accounting and HR roles lend themselves to individual as well as group work. Each student will have different areas to research.

Working in a group

If working in a group, the individual student will still have to demonstrate a 'wide' range of research.

It can be much more difficult if a group want to work together on a dissertation or investigation. However, planning and foresight can prevent problems and allow individual research skills to be identified.

For a dissertation on the slave trade in the eighteenth century by a group of three people, roles can be broken down in this way:

- one person focuses on the slaves
- another concentrates on the slave traders and owners
- the third person looks at the causes and wider impact of the slave trade
- all three contribute to a concluding chapter, demonstrating their ability to work together.

Breaking up the topic in this way gives each member the opportunity to demonstrate the required 'wide range' of research skills/evaluation.

Four people writing a report or investigation into binge-drinking may assign one of the following tasks to each person:

- one person examines the causes of binge-drinking
- another explores its impact on individuals
- a third person look at the impact on communities
- the fourth person considers possible solutions
- all four contribute to a concluding section on the entire issue, demonstrating group skills.

Each member of the group has the opportunity to conduct wide-ranging research and deal with a wide range of different resources.

Working in a group

Build into the planning process of each group project the way in which individuals can meet the assessment criteria.

The person working on the causes of binge-drinking could consider the following types of research:

- Conduct a wide range of primary research, talking to individuals who indulge in binge-drinking, people who own pubs and bars, the police, youth workers, psychologists, journalists, former binge-drinkers who have now 'reformed'.

- Look at secondary sources, ranging from those aimed at the popular market to the highly academic.
- Look at other reports/investigations on the issue by specialists and journalists in a range of publications.

Don't be put off the idea of working with others. Group projects can be very successful, but just remember to consider very carefully the assessment criteria before you begin, and make sure that the assessor can identify the work of each member separately.

Supervisors and specialist advisors

Supervisors

Every school and college will organise supervision in its own way. Do not be put off from your topic if your supervisor is not a specialist in your chosen area, or if there is not an 'expert' in this area in your school. This situation gives you more scope to gain marks for your initiative, enterprise and independence. See it as an opportunity to teach your supervisor something!

Moderator's hint
Having a supervisor who knows nothing about your project topic can be a real advantage.

Some schools quite deliberately allocate students to supervisors whose specialist subjects are far removed from their student's projects; for example, a project on 'animation in film' being supervised by a geography teacher. This encourages the supervisor to focus on ensuring that you meet the criteria and therefore gain marks for skills such as planning and evaluation, rather than worry about whether your views on what makes good animation are correct or not. This also avoids the temptation for the supervisor to take over and dictate the content and planning for you. Your supervisor has a very clearly defined role, so be careful that you do not put your supervisor in the position where, by trying to help you, they actually cost you marks.

Using specialist advisors

You may receive specialist help, either within or outside your school/college. For many projects it would be very unusual if you did not seek such help. You will not lose marks if you use the staff, both teaching and non-teaching, in your school or college to help you do the following:

- Acquire new skills, ranging from project management to communication skills, or how to use Photoshop.
- Point you in the right direction. With an archaeological project, a history teacher might be able to suggest organisations to help you with finding out information about a local area, such as local historical/archaeological societies, records offices and university

departments of archaeology. The business studies department could suggest how to gain information about local or national firms, or how to develop marketing skills.

- Recommend someone who is knowledgeable about your project area. The music department may know little about modern Irish music, but they may point you in the direction of someone who has more knowledge.
- Obtain resources for you. School and college librarians have proved invaluable for previous projects. Librarians are highly trained in information retrieval/search, so make use of their skills.

Moderator's hint
There may be lots of valuable expertise in your school or college: use it!

Outside specialists

You may also consult outside specialists. If you were a project manager deciding where to place a new outlet for a major retail business, you would consult specialists such as planners, consulting engineers, marketing experts and distribution specialists. The same requirement applies to your project.

Take care to ensure that prior to any interview/consultation (which could be face-to-face, by phone or email) that you prepare for your interview carefully so you don't waste his/her time. Think about the following points:

- What information/ideas/opinions are you trying to gain?
- What is the best way of gaining them?
- How will you record this information? Tape? Video? Written notes?
- Check that the specialist is aware that their information is being recorded and agrees to this.
- Have your questions ready.
- If the specialist only has a limited amount of time, make sure that the key questions are asked first.
- Be polite: don't put them off helping someone else like you!

Other points to bear in mind when interviewing or consulting experts:

- Listen carefully. Don't try and impose your own views, even if you don't like what they are saying and disagree strongly.
- Make sure it is all carefully recorded, with correct date and time.
- If you make use of the information gained in your project, then make sure this is noted and properly attributed in the bibliography.
- A brief 'thank you' letter is always a good idea; you want to make life easy for your successors!

Consulting a wide range of experts can enhance your project. Here are some examples of the types of experts students have consulted:

- Skateboard design project: talked to skateboard designers and manufacturers, skateboard championship winners and other users, specialists in general product design, and design engineers.
- Sports coaching techniques project: consulted players, coaches, academics at sports colleges.
- Investigation into the provision of youth services project: talked to youth workers, local government officers and councillors, journalists, academic specialists in local government, local historians.

Moderator's hint
Notice the <u>range</u> of expertise used. This is vital for gaining that A*.

- General Election of 1983 project: talked to voters, politicians, journalists and academics (although there were some reservations about the 'expertise' of some of those in the evaluation!).

All of these students benefited enormously from consulting experts. Using their expertise helped the students to gain high marks in AO2 and AO3.

Moderator's hint
Always remember to review/evaluate any expert views you may get. Remember that 'expert' bankers who made horrendous errors are reckoned to have caused the credit crunch of 2009.

Data collection

Data should be collected, stored and used in an ethical manner. For further details, see the OCR website http://www.ocr.org.uk/qualifications/type/projects/projects/extended/index.aspx. You may need to collect primary data as part of your research, such as finding out how customers viewed a service you have provided, or collecting opinions on a controversial issue such as abortion or faith schools. School/college teachers in the geography or sociology department can give you good advice on how to collect and use data.

HOW TO SUCCEED

Remember that thinking and planning here will pick up AO1 marks.

There are now several cheap and easy-to-use software programmes which will help you collate and evaluate data; your ICT department can help you with this.

HOW TO SUCCEED

Marks are awarded for the acquisition of new skills.

Guidelines on collecting data

Ensure that the objectives of your data collection are clear before you start.

- What information do you want? Is this the only way to find it?
- What do you want to glean from that information?
- How and where will you find it?
- When will you find it?
- Is it sensitive information? Might it be a sensitive issue to other people?
- Will it require confidentiality?
- Does your supervisor know what you are doing and why?
- How can you ensure the reliability of the data?
- How much will it cost?
- Will it involve face-to-face interviews? Email? Telephone? Filling in a questionnaire?
- How will you gather a range of views?
- Does it matter if it is just a random sample, or must it be a genuine cross-section of views?
- How will you find a genuine cross-section of views?

HOW TO SUCCEED

Planning for data collection is vital. Make sure you evaluate both the data collected and the methods used for data collection for your AO4 'review' marks.

Methods of data collection

There are three main ways of collecting data:

1 By **observation**: you simply watch and count, for example:
   - Do people prefer to use a shop which has music playing in it, or not?
   - How many people use the different facilities offered by a public library on a weekday, and on a Saturday?
2 By **survey**:
   - Hand out a questionnaire to individuals or groups, asking for example which factors might have influenced their voting behaviour in the previous general election.
   - Conduct a face-to-face interview asking which type of skateboard was preferred and why.

3 By **experimentation**:
- Run two school discos; one is alcohol-free for a good cause, and the other where alcohol is available, but is run for a profit. Observe the effect on attendance numbers.
- Which type of product will sell better in a market, the one with elaborate packaging or the one without?

Always remember to:

- work out what data you need first
- think about the amount of data you need
- decide how and when you are going to find it
- decide how you are going to evaluate it.

Library skills

Most projects will involve the use of a library at some stage, whether to find a book, a photograph, some data, a map, or official information.

Librarians are trained and skilled specialists in helping people find information. Make use of those skills, as they can be underused. You may find they are delighted to help someone who wishes to make real use of their specialist skills.

Moderator's hint
Make sure that you know how to use a library properly before you start your project.

In addition to a school or college library there are other libraries which may be useful to you.

Public libraries
Public libraries:

- have their own collections of books, maps, prints, local archives
- can access all other public library materials
- can link into academic libraries
- are excellent at helping you find things, and telling you where to look.

Academic libraries

- Every university, training college, and specialist HE institution such as an art college, will have a library and specialist librarians.
- Often much of their material is available online.
- They can be very keen to help potential students.
- They are often aware of specialist teachers in the institution who may be able to help you.

Specialist libraries
There is a staggering range of specialist libraries, with much of their material available online. For example:

- The Wellcome Library of Medical History: this library was extremely helpful for a student doing a project on the history of blood transfusion.
- The British Film Institute Library: a student found this very useful in providing information and resources for a project on the use of 3-D techniques in cinema.

Remember that wide-ranging library skills (beyond knowing where the physics section is in the school library and being able to use a catalogue) are important skills for you to acquire and you will gain credit for doing so.

> **Moderator's hint**
> Knowing how and where to look for specialist information is a great asset.

The Internet

There is plenty of material in other places on using the Internet for research, and with the pace of development, almost anything written in a book like this may be out of date by the time it is published. However, a few basic rules apply:

- Ensure that you have proper training in Internet use before you start, as it can save you a great deal of time.
- Do not rely too much on Internet research.
- Do not put too much faith in the accuracy and reliability of information and ideas found on the Internet.

> **Moderator's hint**
> Effective use of the Internet has led to many good projects.

- Always reference carefully anything you may wish to use. Bibliographies should not contain phrases like, 'found on the Net'.
- There are smaller specialist sites for almost everything, from archaeology to surfboarding; these often prove to be the most valuable.
- Always evaluate carefully the information you get from a site, and double-check it if you can.
- Ration the time carefully you spend using the Internet.

HOW TO SUCCEED

Misuse and overuse of the Internet can prevent you from gaining the high grades.

Statistics/maps/diagrams/photos/illustrations

Your project may involve the considerable use of statistics and many other types of illustration, particularly if it is a report or investigation. Again this is an area where your school/college can give a lot of initial help;

departments such as economics and geography use statistics and illustrations as an integral part of their work.

This may be an area where you have the chance to gain a new skill. However, remember the old saying that there are 'lies, damned lies and statistics'. Be cautious and follow these guidelines:

- Check that the statistics or other data are really relevant to your project. There have been many cases of statistics being included which had little relevance beyond demonstrating the fact that the student had actually done some work.
- Check that they are evidence of your skills, your research or both. They should be relevant to at least one of the four assessment objectives.
- Ensure that all illustrations, charts and sets of figures are relevant and clearly explained, with proper headings. An intelligent non-specialist (such as the moderator) should not have to work out what they are about and why they are included.
- Check that the information is in the best format: would a graph be better as a bar chart? Would the photo benefit from cropping?
- Have you too many or too few figures and illustrations?
- Are you using (manipulating) them to prove your point, or are you drawing a reasoned conclusion from the data? (One of the best projects that this writer has seen was on the use and abuse of statistics.)
- Are they in the right place in your project? Should they be in the main body or at the end? If at the end, does the main body of the report/dissertation direct the reader on where to find them?

Plagiarism

Plagiarism means using work written or created by someone else and presenting it as if it is your own work. One of the key tasks performed by your supervisor and the school/college is to ensure that the project is your own work. They will be monitoring it closely and will have to take responsibility if there is cheating. There is an old saying that 'copying from one book is plagiarism/cheating, while copying from two is research'. The Extended Project expects you to do a lot more than that!

Exam boards and HE institutions see plagiarism as a major offence, and in many instances there have been career-wrecking implications for those who were caught. A few guidelines to avoid being accused of plagiarism:

Moderator's hint
It now takes less than 30 seconds for sophisticated software to track down something copied from the Internet.

- Don't do it.
- Always make it clear when you are using another person's work/ideas/words, etc.
- Don't just copy out whole paragraphs when making notes; summarise in your own words.
- Remember the AO2 requirement about a 'range of resources'.
- Don't try to adapt an old piece of coursework or someone else's project; the moderator will quickly recognise this and you will lose marks.
- Don't ask someone else to write up your project or present it for you. This will be regarded as cheating.
- Keep your supervisor informed of your progress so that s/he knows that it is your own work.

Moderator's hint
The best way to avoid being accused of cheating is to keep your supervisors regularly informed of what **you** are doing and how **you** are doing it.

Assessment Objective 3: Developing and realising

Learning goals

By the end of the chapter you should be able to:

- Select appropriate material to include
- Select and use relevant tools, equipment and techniques
- Make use of the performance outcomes and marking grids
- Manage your project – step by step
- Decide whether to do an individual or group project
- Keep a record of your PLTS, particularly if you are a Diploma student
- Solve problems and develop strategies for success.

The OCR specification

Assessment Objective 3 carries 40 per cent of the total marks.

This assessment objective is about the actual doing and completion of the project, and many marks are awarded for this. These vital marks are allocated primarily for **skills** and not for content.

To achieve full marks for this AO, the student needs to demonstrate that a wide range of skills has been selected and used in a sophisticated manner in order to:

- solve problems
- take decisions
- achieve the planned outcome.

There could be many different skills used, depending on the nature of the project, and they could include:

- problem-solving techniques
- analytical techniques
- PLTS (personal learning and thinking skills) such as
  - reflective learning
  - team-working
  - self-managing
  - effective participation
- functional skills such as
  - communication

- ICT
- maths
- presentation skills
- other technical skills, which could range from computer programming to digital photography or linguistic skills
■ If appropriate, a wide range of appropriate technologies (such as computer-aided design) can be used to help with problem-solving, decision-making and achieving the planned outcome.

Moderator's hint
Notice the constant focus on skills.

To achieve an A* in this AO you will need to do the following:

■ Use a range of different skills to complete your project: for example, communication, ICT, writing, construction, photography, managing people.
■ Demonstrate effectively how those skills were important to complete the project. You may have used one range of skills in the project design and another range in completing the project.

However, you could receive zero marks if you:

■ choose a project which does not demonstrate the use of skills,
■ focus heavily on the content rather than what you did,
■ do not show evidence of the skills gained and used.

Apart from the completed project in whichever format you choose, you need to provide evidence in the form of a commentary describing the skills and/or techniques/technologies used during the planning, development and realisation stages of your work. Keeping **records** is therefore very important.

What you will need to know, or be able to do

(The following is built around the OCR Extended Project Handbook, page 14 onwards (the assessment criteria) and can be downloaded from the OCR website.)

Learning objectives/main points

■ Take control of your learning and development.
■ Ask other people to be 'critical friends' – ask for constructive feedback. Think who would give the best and most honest, supportive answer if you were to ask: 'Does my project look big in this?'
■ What do you need to know, and what don't you need to know?
■ Use your supervisor to help you with the scope of the project.
■ Share ideas with others: learn from multiple sources.
■ Obtain advice and information from your tutors and family, university admissions officers and librarians.

Maintaining a focus on your targets

■ Ensure you understand the performance descriptors.

Moderator's hint
The more you understand what the assessor/moderator is looking for, the more likely you are to produce it.

It is important that you remind yourself of your project's 'question, task or brief' at all times (use Post It notes as a visual reminder).

■ Focus on the 'problem' or the 'title'.
■ Maintain your focus on the title or problem.
■ Good titles and good problems lead to good solutions.

How to achieve a high grade

In Appendix B of the latest OCR specification handbook for the Extended Project there are typical performance criteria for each level of project, with reference to:

1 how to achieve top marks and higher grades
2 the E/U grade boundary

This is now in Appendix B of the latest OCR specification/handbook for the Extended Project.

Moderator's hint
If you are unsure about what AO1, AO2, etc, mean, refer to the specification for this qualification. Ask your tutor/supervisor.

HOW TO SUCCEED

If you fully absorb the following, you will really improve your chances of achieving a high score. Ask your teacher to help with this.

To be judged as a grade E, your work should demonstrate the following, as indicated in the OCR Extended Project Handbook:

■ **AO1**
  • There is limited evidence of personal choice and research into the project title (likely to be rather broad, lacking focus). A basic rationale is given with little real engagement from the candidate.
  • Candidate produces a workable plan, although the objectives lack clarity.

■ **AO2**
  • Project lacks coherent research.
  • A range of resources is used, although not necessarily including the different types expected for the project.
  • There is some evidence of making links and connections to related areas.

■ **AO3**

- There is some evidence of skills development and limited evidence of response to feedback or advice.
- There is a generally logical structure, but some errors in the use of language are likely.
- Candidate partially realises the planned outcomes.
- There is a broad set of conclusions, but very little in the way of analysis.

■ **AO4**

- There is some review of the way the final outcomes have emerged from the objectives and to own learning and performance.
- The presentation is generally effective but may lack coherence and/or complete accuracy.
- Responses to questions reveal some knowledge and understanding of the topic area.

Source: *OCR Extended Project Handbook* (2009)

You should aim for the following, which is the typical performance criteria set out to help assessors and moderators recognise the work of the A* candidates, as indicated on page 59 of the *OCR Extended Project Handbook*:

■ **AO1**

- Candidate personally develops the project title and phrases it as a clearly focused question, hypothesis or brief, and provides a clear rationale for the project.
- Candidate personally identifies appropriate strategies, tasks and objectives, justifies his/her choices and engages with them.
- The work is well-planned, well-organised and coherent, and includes appropriate autonomous review and modification.

■ **AO2**

- A rich and varied range of sources of information is used critically and effectively, and resources are used appropriately.
- Research skills, technical language and/or specialist vocabulary are evident and well-developed.
- There is evidence of clear understanding of the complexities of the topic.
- There is evidence of synthesis through the making of relevant links to related areas.

■ AO3

- There is considered response to guidance and evidence of critical reflection, plus appropriate action on advice given.
- There is reference to problems encountered and justification of action taken to address these.
- There is evidence of the development of skills, including underpinning ideas and concepts where appropriate, and of clear understanding of the topic area.
- Candidate achieves a high quality and appropriate outcome that realises most of the intentions of the project.

■ AO4

- The candidate carries out an in-depth evaluation in relation to stated objectives and to own learning and performance. Reasons for any non-realisation of objectives are identified, as are any flaws in the original objectives.
- The outcomes of the project are clearly presented, including explicit commentary on findings and conclusions that are clearly related to the original objectives.
- The candidate makes use of a range of appropriate presentation skills.
- The candidate responds well to questions and displays a clear and in-depth knowledge and understanding of the topic area.

Source: *OCR Extended Project Handbook* (2009)

What you need to know and/or do before starting your project

The following is taken from page 15 of the OCR Extended Project Handbook:

Topic and type of outcome may go hand in hand, so your first task is to decide on a few ideas for projects that you could do to enhance your Diploma study or help prepare for your progression into work or a higher level of learning.

If you intend progressing to university:

- What project could you undertake to help prepare you for this?
- If you are aiming for a particular university, what would impress them? (but don't just do it to impress)
- If you show research ability, not many universities would want to turn you away.

- Have you decided what you want to study at university? If not, this is an essential place to start – the type of degree you want determines how you prepare for entry.
- Start any planning with the end product – the outcome – and aim for it.

If your intention is to find a job or an apprenticeship:

- Can you decide on a project that will help make you more employable than someone else?
- Do you know someone, perhaps at your place of work experience, who could help you focus on an idea?
- Think about how your studies on the Diploma or other qualification can be supported or enhanced by carrying out an effective and relevant project which will help prepare you for work in your chosen industry or with a particular employer.

Once you have come up with a few ideas:

- Bounce them around with your friends, family and tutor(s).
- Look through the Extended Project assessment grids and negotiate with your tutor to ensure that your project idea(s) have the potential to cover the full set of learning outcomes across all three mark bands.
- Again, this is focusing on the outcome or end product of your project.
- The assessment grid and mark bands should be seen as your guide to help you set your targets so that you achieve the maximum marks and other benefits from carrying out your project.

Focus on the project which best suits:

- you
- your method of working
- the time available
- your intentions
- the support of your tutor or supervisor
- previous knowledge of the topic, etc.

Start to define the aims:

- Exactly what is it that you intend to achieve?
- What are you aiming for?
- What are your intended outcomes?
- Will it be acceptable to your intended audience?
- Are you aiming to do a dissertation or make something?
- Or are you aiming to work on a topic or subject and let the 'type' of outcome grow?

Ask someone else to check your ideas and see if they agree that they address the full set of mark bands. If not, what is missing? Does anything need removing or rewriting?

Moderator's hint
Once you have got this far, you are well on the way to addressing the first learning outcome. This accounts for about 20 per cent of the marks, or 12 out of 60. The marking grid will clearly show this.

This reflective style of working always leads to personal improvement: have an idea, plan what to do, carry it out, reflect on what you did and evaluate how well it went, review it, decide how it could be done better, carry it out, reflect, evaluate, etc.

The next steps

Planning

Now you have a project title and you've almost decided on a style of outcome. Imagine your project as a journey. Completing the project will be your last step, and your plan will be your first. Plan out everything you think you may need to do, find out, learn, write, make, change, check or ask; and put them in order. This can be done using a diagram, a flow chart or a list of ideas, depending on your own learning style. You may find Gantt charts or critical path networks helpful, either on paper or on a computer. If not, do it your own way.

This is your project and your skills will be assessed for effectiveness, not necessarily for doing as you are told and following other people's patterns and ideas.

Mindmaps can be useful; you could include one or two in the project to show your thoughts and plans. If you prefer the linear approach, use a simple timeline; draw a line across the middle of a landscape piece of A4 paper, and add the main points which you aim to cover from start to finish.

Whatever planning methods you use, they all help to put your plans in order and show you what needs to be done, when, and in what order.

Moderator's hint
Remember, you are assessed on managing the project, not its content.

If you start your project without planning, you may rapidly discover that you need more information than you imagined, which may jeopardise your timeline plans.

Use the SMART system in setting targets:
- Specific – say exactly what you aim to do.
- Measurable – if you can't measure progress, how do you know that you have moved?
- Achievable – it must be within your grasp and ability.

- Realistic – don't set out to change the world, just part of yours.
- Time bound – capable of being done in the time given.

You could even be SMARTER by adding these two points:

- Effective – your work on the project should be more than just passing time.
- Results – after spending time on your project, you will have something to show for your efforts.

No doubt you could make one up to be SMARTEST?

Research

The second learning outcome states that you must be able to plan and carry out independent research, either individually or as part of a collaborative group. This is easy to identify if you are working on your own on an individual project, with a little guidance. If a few of you decide that you want, or need, to work together on a collaborative project, what evidence could you produce to prove that you worked independently as part of a group? How can you work individually in a group?

Think of a team activity. This could be a physical team sport, such as climbing or pot-holing, rugby or football, or it could be taking part in a play, playing an instrument in an orchestra or singing in a band or choir. It could be for the manufacture of an item, such as a car or bicycle. Table 6 shows the individual parts played in some of these instances. The first two are completed: can you complete the others?

Individual team member	Team/group	Part played in the team
Scrum half	Rugby team	Puts the ball into a scrum and retrieves it, starting play along a line of players.
Bass guitarist	Rock band	Plays the bass notes which may hold the rhythm or style to complement the other players.
Tyre manufacturer	Motor car or motor cycle production	
Anchor	Tug of war team	
Triangle player	Orchestra	
Checkout operator	Supermarket	
Hole digger	Three hole diggers	

Table 6 Individual parts of team activities

In fact, it seems that almost everything we do makes us part of a team, or perhaps several teams.

Table 6 also indicates how individuals may benefit from others within a collaborative project. One member of your team may find something useful for another team member, identifying what is relevant to their project aims and outcomes, and passing it on to someone else who can also evaluate its usefulness (this could be good evidence for the PLTS – see Assessment Objective 3).

This would effectively address the assessment criteria for the second learning outcome, to use a wide and appropriate range of sources of information and select methods to collect information which are relevant to your task or individual research. It would also be collating information from a range of sources and evaluating these for suitability of purpose and quality.

Information gathering from a wide range of sources

If you were to ask the question, 'how wide is a wide range?', the best answer you could expect is 'wide enough to inform you based on the requirements of the Extended Project'. How long is a piece of string? The only accurate answer is 'twice half its length'. As in the case of the project, the actual length of string needed depends on what you will use it for. If you wanted to string two conkers, a metre of string cut in half would be enough for both. How long a piece of string would you need to knit a vest?

In other words, every project requires a varying range of sources of information, and you have to select methods of collecting information which are relevant to the task.

Hence, if you haven't planned properly, identifying and listing the tasks which you will carry out from start to finish, or at least written a few of them down, you cannot start to determine the range of sources you might need to access.

Collating the information

After conducting lots of research such as Internet searches, reading books, and talking to a few people, you will have much information. Does this prove your research ability? No, it proves that you have lots of information. You need to pull it together, sift through it for relevance, and keep a record of the sources for referencing.

EVIDENCE
Keep a record or provide evidence to show how you selected the most suitable material for inclusion.

KEEPING RECORDS

✓ Keeping records allows you or an assessor to go back and check your reference. It also recognises the source as being informative and helping to shape your own work, and someone may one day use and reference your work.

You can collate the relevant information by keeping notes and records on cards (just like revision cards) and keeping them in some sort of order; or it can be done electronically allowing automatic search, filter and sort actions. Monitor your own research progress:

- Before you start, try to estimate what you need to be achieving every two to three weeks.
- Regularly monitor and evaluate your progress.
- Become self-critical, in a supportive way; try not to be self-destructive.
- This allows you to change direction, research methods, or even your mind about your project, including the final overall outcome or type of project. You may set out to make something, but become so interested in the background or history of the product's needs that you decide to do a dissertation or an investigation into this instead.
- Be ruthless with your research findings and evaluate the information: if the material or information which you gather is not relevant to your stated aims or the project in general, why are you keeping it? However, don't discard or delete the information yet, just in case you need to refer to it later. If you are doing a group project, your discarded information may provide a useful lead for someone else.

Effective use of resources earns up to around 20 per cent of the overall marks (approximately another 12 marks out of 60), which now means that you are almost halfway towards completion.

EVIDENCE

A moderator will check your work by post. Ensure that you have documented how you selected and used the resources and equipment, or you will not be awarded marks for non–evident ephemeral evidence. Remember also to state how you evaluated the helpfulness or usefulness of your sources of information.

Develop and realise the project

(This information about Assessment Outcome 3 is taken from the Extended Project Handbook, p 15.

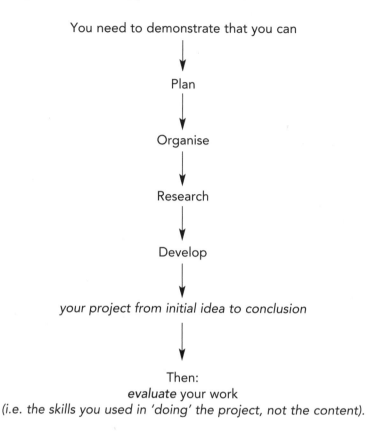

You need to demonstrate that you can

Plan

Organise

Research

Develop

your project from initial idea to conclusion

Then:
evaluate your work
(i.e. the skills you used in 'doing' the project, not the content).

Figure 2 Demonstrating your skills

Evidence

Each of these component activities must be supported by evidence. If no evidence exists, even if your tutor/supervisor witnesses your work all the way through from start to finish, how can a remote moderator agree that your work has been assessed fairly and accurately? If your future employer or university admissions tutor wants to see the evidence, and all you have is a final score and no material for him or her to judge, all your work may have been wasted. Keep your evidence, ensuring that it is valid and well referenced. Your tutor/supervisor should be able to provide some guidance on how you can evidence all aspects of your work.

Take a professional approach to developing your own learning and project management skills. Part of the planning process will require you to decide on your research methodology. A quick Internet search for 'research methodology' will provide a long list of pointers; you need to evaluate which sites are useful and which are wrong or trying to sell you something. You need to decide which sources to investigate, and determine which are providing you with the best and most relevant advice for your project, your own research or your investigation.

How to record the evidence

If you have a meeting or discussion with others, it is very difficult to write down everything you say. How can you keep a record of the discussion?

Many electronic devices are available to provide an electronic recording, and most mobile phones or computers incorporate sound recording facilities. Be cautious however, because although most people will not mind such a recording taking place, if you do not ask them first and explain why you are doing this, they may be offended.

Don't forget to evidence your use of the recording technology within your project.

How to submit the evidence

- You could transfer the evidence to a CD or DVD, or place it on a VLE and provide access authority for your tutor/supervisor.
- Alternatively, you could write a transcript of the recording, or you may be able to 'train' your computer to your voice(s) and record your discussion directly into a word processor. (You should however read it carefully afterwards.) This will allow identification of the speakers taking part in the discussion and printouts to add to your portfolio, as well as allowing easy access for reading, marking or moderating.
- You could ask the participants in your discussion if they would mind checking the transcript for accuracy, and even sign it to say so; this is good authentication evidence for your work.

Timescales: keeping on track

Many projects begin with the best of intentions, but fail to reach completion due to lack of project management skills. Students may complain that they ran out of time, but this is not right: they gave themselves too much to do and did not manage their workload.

Schedule your time

Discipline yourself to devote a specific amount of time to your project on a regular basis. Do not be tempted to spend a full day on the project, and then leave it for several days or weeks hoping to pick it back up. You will waste time in revisiting all the work to remind you of your thoughts; you might even start amending the first part to add your new thoughts, then find that you've already added these new thoughts in a later part.

Summarise

As you complete each section of work, or as you approach the end of your allocated time slot, spend a couple of minutes summarising what you plan to do next and the work you have done so far.

When you next visit the work, if you can't interpret your summary or plan for the next step, what chance would someone have of assessing your work when you have completed all of it?

If you are working through a book or website, and summarising some details to use within your project, note the source and the specific page/line where you have finished off before leaving it. This allows you to come straight back to the work and quickly resume work.

In order to be awarded marks for carrying out such good practices, you need to clearly evidence what you did and how you did it. To support this more, you could evaluate how effectively you carried the activities out in your final review and evaluation.

Plan the timing for each step of the project

An important part of your planning should have been estimating the time it will take you to carry out each step of your project. Remember however that this is a plan and plans change. If you realise that you have spent too long on one aspect, modify the others.

Moderator's hint
If a project is submitted and the planned timing is totally accurate for every aspect of the work, this usually indicates that the plan was not completed until after the work had been completed.

When planning the timings, start at the end and estimate how long the final activity might take? You might need to allow three to four weeks for the final write-up.

Before that, all your notes and ideas should have been arranged, following their collection. The estimate of time for these may have been four to six weeks, and so on.

It will soon become apparent that if for example there are eight activities and each takes three to four weeks, the total project duration would be fairly stated as exactly somewhere between 24 and 32 weeks.

The end time should be seen as set in stone and immovable. Although each of the steps has some allowed tolerance, the final deadline for handing in cannot be moved; actions may need to overlap, sections may need to be missed out, certain steps might have to be cut and even omitted altogether.

Deciding which parts to skim over or omit depends on the type of project you are doing, but this will help develop your project management skills. You should not just 'cut corners' for the sake of it, but consider the outstanding work. Think carefully about whether some parts are achievable or might be effectively reduced without losing too many marks, and work on reducing your project requirements to fit the remaining time.

Group projects

A key challenge when managing a group project is to avoid total disaster if one or more members of the group does not keep up with the work plan. Below are guidelines for a group of three people producing an artefact or performance as their project.

Serial or sequential activities

Making an item which consists of several serial activities, each dependent on the previous one being completed, would not be recommended.

If the work was shared out very fairly and all had an equal workload, but one of the team does not complete one of their activities or steps, it is impossible to continue.

The work could be shared out again, but research may not have been conducted to adequately complete that part, so potential disaster looms.

Parallel or combinational activities

- Each person would have a range of tasks and activities allocated to them, and they could be monitored against the planned timescale, with adjustments and extra support added where needed, to ensure completion of the overall project.
- The team could elect a leader (good team working skills – see Assessment Objectives 3, the PLTS).
- The team members could share the leader's role, perhaps for a month at a time.

If one or more of the team members were unable to complete their part, for whatever reason, the rest of the team should each at least stand a chance of completing their part of the project and achieving a reasonably high score, where deserved.

Your supervisor will discuss this with you before you start your project.

 Task

Consider the following group project ideas and discuss the points raised.

Building a motorcycle tricycle

One team member is making and painting the frame and front forks; another is preparing the engine, gearbox and mounting brackets; and the final team member is fitting the handlebars, seat, petrol tank, wheels and drive mechanism.

* What could happen if the team member who was making the frame and forks became ill or moved schools, and became unable to continue with the project?
* How would the other two team members be affected?
* What could they do to ensure they had a reasonable chance of accumulating a high project score?

Forming a music band

Four students decide to put together a band and write their own songs for a 30 minute performance to raise money for a charity.

* They all work together to write the music and words.
* Individually, the singer and the three instrumentalists all prepare for a short solo during the performance.
* If the singer becomes ill and is unable to take part in the performance concert, how could this affect the results of other team members?
* How could good project management techniques be used to ensure that they all had a good chance of achieving a high score?

Climate change report

A group of three students is concerned about claims in the media of temperature changes, and decides to produce a timeline of the climatic conditions of the Earth.

* One will investigate the records of weather patterns.
* Another will research the industrial influence on climate change.
* The third will study spot cycles in the sun.
* The project aim is to produce a picture of these phenomena over the last two centuries, or even further back if time permits.

While studying the sun's spot cycles, an interesting article is found which suggests that the Earth's own interior volcanic actions may have an erratic influence on the Earth's climate. Discuss whether and how this can be incorporated, and how the team can share out the work to ensure that they all have opportunities to achieve their potential.

Working with others

This information covers Learning Outcome 4 of the third assessment Criteria (working with others: selecting and using tools and equipment, solving problems).

Managing a project requires a broad range of skills. Project managers continue to develop these skills throughout their careers, so it is not expected that your work will be perfect in this respect yet.

As technology has changed from using massive paper Gantt charts for major projects, electronic methods have been developed, such as Microsoft Projects. Using this program is not however essential for completing your project (although learning how to use it effectively might make a good topic for the Extended Project, and an appropriate title might be 'Microsoft Projects – a critical analysis of the learner-friendliness of this software tool').

Managing a project involves many problem-solving skills, because as in real life, things rarely go to plan.

The PLTS

If you are studying the Diploma alongside the Extended Project, you will be aware of the need to evidence the PLTS, or the 'personal learning and thinking skills'. Even if you are taking the Extended Project as a stand-alone qualification, it would be worthwhile looking at the PLTS to see the range of skills which you will be using and developing.

The PLTS are skills which are generally covered in your work, but not recorded as evidence, so it is a good idea to keep a record of how you cover the PLTS, whether for the Diploma or to demonstrate to a university admissions tutor or future employer that you can monitor your own working methods and reflect on things that you learn or need to learn, solve problems and identify skills which are needed in all vocational and personal aspects of life.

What are the PLTS?

The PLTS exist in many guises: transferable skills, common skills, essential skills, work skills, etc. Some employers refer to these as 'soft skills', but such terminology is not derogatory, in fact quite the contrary. Employers have complained that new recruits do not have some of the skills required to become part of an effective workforce. New employees are sometimes unaware of how to work in teams or develop themselves into effective participators or independent inquirers.

Many teachers, lecturers and students would disagree with this. Students may have taken part in effective teams, demonstrated effective research skills and held responsible positions in the cadets, scouts, action groups, etc.

Recording PLTS will provide evidence to demonstrate to employers that these skills have been taught, developed, improved and recorded. (You may want to refer to the QCA website http://www.qca.org.uk/qca_13476.aspx, which outlines each section of the PLTS in more detail.)

Task

Using the Extended Project Handbook (pp. 40–41), identify which part(s) can be reasonably expected to generate evidence to address the PLTS outcome statements by placing a tick or cross in each box in Table 7.

	Manage the project	Use resources	Develop and realise	Review your work
Independent enquirer: young people process and evaluate information in their investigations, planning what to do and how to go about it. They take informed and well-reasoned decisions, recognising that others have different beliefs and attitudes.				
IE1 Identify questions to answer and problems to resolve				
IE2 Plan and carry out research, appreciating the consequences of decisions				
IE3 Explore issues, events or problems from different perspectives				
IE4 Analyse and evaluate information, judging its relevance and value				
IE5 Consider the influence of circumstances, beliefs and feelings on decisions and events				
IE6 Support conclusions, using reasoned arguments and evidence				
Team worker: young people work confidently with others, adapting to different contexts and taking responsibility for their own part. They listen to and take account of different views. They form collaborative relationships, resolving issues to reach agreed outcomes.				
TW1 Collaborate with others to work towards common goals				
TW2 Reach agreements, managing discussions to achieve results				
TW3 Adapt behaviour to suit different roles and situations				
TW4 Show fairness and consideration to others				

TW5 Take responsibility, showing confidence in themselves and their contribution				
TW6 Provide constructive support and feedback to others				

Creative thinker: young people think creatively by generating and exploring ideas, making original connections. They try different ways to tackle a problem, working with others to find imaginative solutions and outcomes that are of value.

CT1 Generate ideas and explore possibilities				
CT2 Ask questions to extend their thinking				
CT3 Connect their own and others' ideas and experiences in inventive ways				
CT4 Question their own and others' assumptions				
CT5 Try out alternatives or new solutions and follow ideas through				
CT6 Adapt ideas as circumstances change				

Effective participator: young people actively engage with issues that affect them and those around them. They play a full part in the life of their school, college, workplace or wider community by taking responsible action to bring improvements for others as well as themselves.

EP1 Discuss issues of concern, seeking resolution where needed				
EP2 Present a persuasive case for action				
EP3 Propose practical ways forward, breaking these down into manageable steps				
EP4 Identify improvements that would benefit others as well as themselves				
EP5 Try to influence others, negotiating and balancing diverse views to reach workable solutions				
EP6 Act as an advocate for views and beliefs that may differ from their own				

Self manager: young people organise themselves, showing personal responsibility, initiative, creativity and enterprise with a commitment to learning and self-improvement. They actively embrace change, responding positively to new priorities, coping with challenges and looking for opportunities.				
SM1 Seek out challenges or new responsibilities and show flexibility when priorities change				
SM2 Work towards goals, showing initiative, commitment and perseverance				
SM3 Organise time and resources, prioritising actions				
SM4 Anticipate, take and manage risks				
SM5 Deal with competing pressures, including personal and work-related demands				
SM6 Respond positively to change, seeking advice and support when needed				
Reflective learner: young people evaluate their strengths and limitations, setting themselves realistic goals with criteria for success. They monitor their own performance and progress, inviting feedback from others and making changes to further their learning.				
RL1 Assess themselves and others, identifying opportunities and achievements				
RL2 Set goals with success criteria for their development and work				
RL3 Review progress, acting on the outcome				
RL4 Invite feedback and deal positively with praise, setbacks and criticism				
RL5 Evaluate experiences and learning to inform future progress				
RL6 Communicate their learning in relevant ways for different audiences				

Table 7 The PLTS

Problem-solving

What do you do when faced with a problem? Try to analyse your own reactions when you are faced with something unexpected.

Fill in Table 8, detailing your reaction to different problems.

Moderator's hint

Use Table 7 to record your PLTS and their development throughout your project. These could be completed on a monthly or termly basis, to demonstrate any potential progression and improvement in your PLTS throughout your work on the Extended Project.

Problem	How would you react, and what would you do to solve the problem?
Your favourite television programme is just about to start and there is a power cut.	
You arrive at a restaurant and find that your table has been double-booked.	
You have written down an assignment hand-in date incorrectly, and your teacher/ lecturer asks for it a week before you expected.	
You are travelling to a venue 50 miles away, but the car has broken down, the trains are delayed by three hours because of signal problems and the last bus has just departed.	

Table 8 Dealing with problems

Task

Now discuss these problems with a friend to see if they have a similar or different response. Also ask them if they would have expected you to do what you have written above.

Being a good team player

Do you have a particular role in a team which you always assume, or do you play different parts depending on the team activity being undertaken? Most of us tend to adopt our most comfortable position when working with others, but we all need to step out of our comfort zones occasionally to see how we perform under different conditions.

- Do you like to lead, or follow?
- Do you like to start different things, or complete everything in detail before going on to something else?
- Do you like to select a job to do for the team, or are you happy to be given any task to help the team succeed?
- Are there certain types of people whom you like to take charge of, and are there certain types of people to whom you are happy to listen as they tell you what to do?
- Do you like to be listened to, or would you rather someone else did all the talking?
- If your team does not win or achieve their goals, do you look for someone to blame, or do you consider what you could have done to help bring about a positive conclusion?

If you don't know the answers to these questions before you start this project, you will find out sooner or later, especially if you undertake a group project. If you don't know the answers before you start a group project, should you undertake a project on your own?

If you feel that you are totally lost for ideas, who would you ask in the group? Do you find a particular teacher helpful, or could you approach a number of teachers for advice if your project came to a grinding halt or you didn't know what to do next?

Summary of learning outcomes for AO3

- Maintain a focus.
- Remember that you have a time and word limit.
- Keep the project realistic and achievable.
- Although the content matters to you, it is the process which is assessed.
- Keep focused on project skills.
- Keep the project at the correct level – ensure that your project remains at Level 3.
- PLTS: these are six generic skills associated with the Diploma. They are a key feature of the Principal Learning, but can also be evidenced, and put to use within your project work. Each of the 6 PLTS has a specific set of outcomes.

Assessment Objective 4: Reviewing the project

Learning goals

By the end of the chapter you should be able to:

■ Review and reflect on your project work
■ Write effective summaries
■ Analyse and use feedback
■ Conclude and evaluate your work.

The OCR specification

This assessment objective carries 20 per cent of the total marks.

This tends to be the neglected one of the assessment objectives, as it can become rushed at the end. However the skills required for this criteria are valuable for you and prized by universities and employers.

The first part of each point below is taken straight from the OCR specification, the rules which govern the Extended Project. The examiners will be looking at this document when they are allocating marks to your work. If you meet those objectives in full then you are entitled to full marks. The text in brackets afterwards explains the different points more fully.

To get full marks for this assessment objective you will need to:

Demonstrate an incisive, critical, reflective and independent approach to learning.

(Keep it all as brief and as relevant as you can. Analyse the strengths and weaknesses of all that you are doing carefully and systematically. Demonstrate that you clearly thought about your learning curve throughout the project, and make it obvious that it is **your** work.)

Present a perceptive, thorough and accurate review of your work, covering all aspects from the early ideas/planning stage right the way through to completion.

(Review the whole project thoroughly and make sure that you provide evidence for it.)

Do it as part of a group where it will relate to your participation in a group project.

(Make sure that your contribution to the group project is carefully evaluated, by both you, other group members, and the supervisor. See the BBC television programme 'The Apprentice' for examples of peer review.)

Use both a sophisticated and wide range of communication skills and media to present a perceptive, effective and comprehensive review of the development and outcome of the whole project.

(Think very carefully about the presentation; what are you trying to demonstrate?)

Do a presentation which has met and exceeded the needs of both a specialist and/or non-specialist audience, which was well engaged.

(Keep your presentation interesting and engaging; do not bore your audience. Deal well with all types of questions, particularly those which demonstrate your skills and topic knowledge.)

Show they have addressed clearly and realistically the issue of personal, academic and career development beyond the confines, but informed by, their participation in the project, including their development of transferable skills. They clearly understand what has been achieved and where it can lead them.

(You have understood the whole purpose of undertaking the Extended Project.)

To gain an A* you will need to do the following:

■ Have an absolutely clear record which shows that you have met the objectives. **You** have to provide the evidence.
■ Do a form of presentation where you can be grilled by both experts and non-experts on all aspects of the project, and deal well with all the questions.
■ Use a good range of communication skills to convey to others what you have achieved and how you have achieved it; do not just read out bits of a PowerPoint presentation.
■ You must really show that you have thought about your work and evaluated it seriously.

However, you will receive zero marks for this criteria if you:

■ don't review your project properly,
■ don't provide the evidence that you have reviewed it,
■ dictate to an audience what you have written on a couple of PowerPoint presentations,
■ don't use your presentation to demonstrate the range of skills looked for, and

■ don't answer questions about your project satisfactorily.

This is an area where you will have to take enormous care with your evidence. In the past, several potentially outstanding projects did not achieve the highest grades because of lack of evidence in this area. You will have to provide good evidence of:

■ what you have learned (either to do or to avoid in future)
■ your thinking about the whole project from the very beginning
■ how and why you had the basic idea
■ how well you translated that idea into a manageable project
■ how you dealt with problems
■ how you learned new skills.

HOW TO SUCCEED

Remember that intelligent use of the presentation can be vital to demonstrate that you have done all of these things.

How to evaluate and review

Moderator's hint
Before the moderator assesses your project, you need to have a good look at it as well.

Your supervisor will assess your work, and it will be externally moderated by the awarding body (i.e. OCR).

It is always difficult to read something which you have written, especially if you laboured over it over a long period. You know every part of your own work and when you see each title, you remember the anguish (and some pleasure, hopefully) it caused. You may assume that you know what you have written, so you don't read it properly.

Some possible solutions follow:

■ Ask a friend or parent to read it to you. Listening to a piece of work is very different from reading it.
■ Critical reflection is essential: reflect on what you have done, how you did it, how useful it was, how you could have done it better.
■ Have another look at the PLTS (such as being a 'reflective learner') for ideas about reviewing your work.
■ Try to mark your own efforts to see what score you might be awarded. If you're not sure about any of the contents in the marking grids for your Extended Project, ask your supervisor. S/he is allowed to explain the contents (which are written in rather academic language) and your

understanding of them is essential for you to complete an effective Extended Project.

Experiential learning

No doubt you will have had a range of learning experiences, and you will have learned from these. Some of the things we learn help us to stay alive, but generally we learn from our actions and tend to modify the way we behave in future.

When carrying out the Extended Project, you will be applying this theme of experiential learning. To achieve the best score, it needs to be documented, and the outcomes are written to reflect this.

For example, if you plan to read several parts of a range of books, ask a few people for their opinions, then make notes. You may then consider the information which you have obtained and decide whether or not it is useful. After reflecting on the information and evaluating its usefulness, you may then modify your plan or plan to do something else; then you may carry out this plan, obtain more results, or see the effects of your actions; then review and evaluate, etc.

Put into its simplest terms, the cycle you are going through is:

- reflect
- review
- plan
- apply.

This cycle can be used to describe any learning experience. Questions which occur to you might include the following:

- Have I done something like this before?
- Do the skills I have enable me to do it?
- Do I need to learn something new?

To answer these questions, you may need to do the following:

- Reflect on the task at hand and how it relates to your previous experiences.
- Review how your previous experiences and knowledge worked last time you applied them, and how you may need to modify them for the new experience.
- Plan how you will implement these reviews and what you will do; when, how, and in what order.
- Apply the plan and prepare to reflect on the results again, after you see the outcome of your actions.

Summary writing

Writing a summary is another essential skill which is required for effective project work. You may need to:

- summarise some of your research findings to include in your project report
- write a summary for the introduction to your project report
- summarise your project because it has become too long.

The way in which you summarise will depend on the type of project outcome you have chosen. It will also help to determine the success and effectiveness of your summary.

If you are faced with summarising several thousand words from a book, or content from a few websites, you have a choice of how you approach this task. Doing the following will gain few marks:

- Work through a piece of work a sentence at a time, removing some words or replacing a few words with fewer, but still saying substantially the same thing.
- Work through each paragraph trying to combine sentences together by removing or replacing a few words.

However, a more successful approach will gain high marks:

- Familiarise yourself with the whole work which you are going to summarise.
- Read a section, then write a very short précis of what you have just read.
- Compare your précis with the section to check that you have extracted the main points without including too much detail.

Alternatively:
- Write a sentence to summarise each paragraph.
- Then write an overall sentence to replace your summary sentences, three or four at a time.
- Keep going until you have a succinct summary.

Feedback

Feedback can be defined as that part of a circular or cyclic system or process where the results or output are sampled and directed back for comparison with the input.

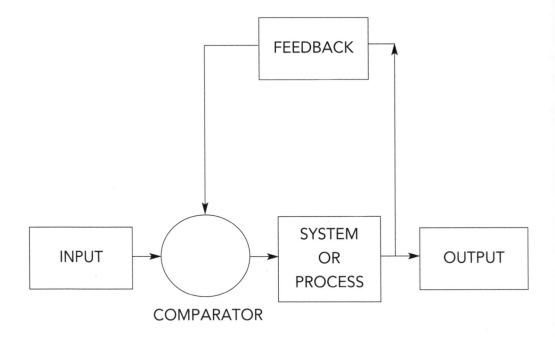

Figure 3 A simple example of a feedback system

Look at Figure 3, which shows a simple feedback system. The output only occurs as a response to some input. The output is produced by the operations within the system or process. The input is where the desired conditions are set. The output also has a 'feed back' to the circular symbol, called a 'comparator'. This 'feedback' loop tells the system how close the output is to the desired input request.

The input and feedback are compared by the comparator and if the output is not quite what is required, the system or process continues to change until the output achieves the desired state.

In the case of the Extended Project:

- input = all your hard work
- system = the Extended Project
- feedback = opinions from you, your tutor or anyone else
- comparator = is it what you wanted or needed?

Feedback on your thoughts, plans and effort will help you retain your focus, with occasional adjustment, and help you see the Extended Project to its completion.

Feedback from supervisors and universities

You will have the option of receiving support from your tutor/supervisor throughout your Extended Project, and you may find other people to discuss things with or to bounce your ideas off. This is permissible as long as supervisors only discuss issues and give you advice about what you could try or where you could research, and do not give you the answers to the criteria across the mark bands. A danger of asking your tutor or a specialist teacher is that they may give you the answer by telling you what to do and what to write. This is malpractice, could lead to a zero score, and does not prepare you for a life full of problem-solving.

You may be applying to go to university. Take your ideas with you and ask the admissions tutor for some feedback. He or she will see you as a researcher, and the potential for university entrance and acceptance could hinge on the fact that you are carrying out research, which is seen as excellent preparation for university study.

University study will involve research, so you will be well prepared; don't be hesitant or discouraged from asking for feedback. Referring to your Extended Project during a UCAS application and during an admissions interview should be seen as a two-way interview – it may influence your decision about where you want to study, as well as helping the university to decide on whether or not to offer you a place.

Feedback from friends

Another good source of feedback is from your peers, friends or classmates. Before asking anyone for their opinions, ask yourself this: 'Will he or she give honest feedback to help me reflect on my work, without offending me?' Could you take positive criticism, without losing that friend?

If so, explain to them what you are doing because the Extended Project might be a new concept to them. Also tell them what kind of feedback you want them to give after they have read it or listened to your explanation about your plans.

You are seeking feedback to help you gain a high score; as long as friends provide positive criticism without telling you exactly what to do, this will be useful in helping you to learn.

Moderator's hint
Be selective about who you ask for feedback. Don't ask too many people: you may run out of time, and have too many different, perhaps contradictory responses.
If someone offers feedback to you and you don't agree with it, say so (nicely) and thank them for their efforts. You can ignore their advice if you want to, after careful evaluation of what they have said.

Drawing conclusions

(This information covers Learning Outcome 5 of Assessment Criteria 5: draw conclusions, analyse and evaluate the outcomes, give a presentation to your pre-determined audience.)

As the project nears completion, you need to maintain your focus on the plan as well as the topic. Final activities should include the following:

- Draw relevant conclusions from your work.
- Analyse the outcomes of your project.
- Evaluate the work you have done and your project management skills.
- Present your final outcome to a relevant audience.

You should also provide evidence to show that you know why these activities are important for a project to be effective and successful.

Draw relevant conclusions from your work

- By referring back to your stated aims and the intended outcomes of the project.
- If you changed your plans along the way, and the changes affected the planned outcomes, refer to them as well.
- Match each point of your outcome with your results.
- Did you arrive at unexpected results? Is this because you missed something, or did you achieve an extra result which was unexpected?

Once you have identified the main conclusions, write a formal analysis of how well you met the outcomes.

Analyse the outcomes of your project

- Once you have completed the other parts of your project, consider the results.
- Your teacher will be assessing the work, which is a different task to the one which you now have to carry out.
- The student's evaluation needs documenting as it forms the last outcome for which marks will be awarded.
- Are your results and findings as expected?
- Did you find anything extraordinary?
- Have you recorded all sources of information – books, websites, magazines, journals, talking to people, etc?

Moderator's hint
Remember that the contents of your project are not being assessed. Concentrate your final efforts on analysing and evaluating the results of your project.

Evaluate the work you have done and your project management skills

- Did you keep a record of any changes to the timing of your activities throughout this project?
- Did you change your plans halfway through?
- Have you done as much as you expected?
- Did it take more time than expected or allowed?
- What is the word count for your project?
- Did you make something, or do an investigation?
- Did you meet your aims and objectives, including any amended ones?
- If you were to assess your own work against the mark bands, how many points would you give yourself? (Doing this fairly will give you a good idea of anything that is missing.)
- How effective do you think you have been at managing this project?
- For a group project: have all the members identified who did what?
- Did anything in particular hold you back or cause problems?
- Did you find any particular source of information more helpful than others?

Present your final outcome to a relevant audience

- How long have you been considering the format of your presentation?
- Will it be a performance, such as a play or a musical presentation?
- Is your main project a large written piece? If so, how will you make it concise enough to present to your audience?
- If you have made something, did it work? (Remember that this does not affect the project score.)
- With an artefact or model, the written part can be shorter but long enough to explain the project to a reader (assessor or moderator).
- Will you need to use a projector, such as for a PowerPoint presentation?
- What other presentation methods have you considered?
- Why did you choose the method which you intend to use?
- How often have you rehearsed or practised giving similar presentations?

Audience reaction

- You need to consider how you will record the feedback from your audience.
- Will you use a questionnaire?
- Will you give them a checklist with boxes to write in?
- How will you feel if they give you bad news?
- You need to evidence the audience responses and ask them to verify their comments.

- This feedback will be used to form part of your formal assessed score, but so will your responses and analysis of the feedback.
- If you know what went wrong, explain this; you are not expected to be perfect.
- You will be assessed on what you communicate and how you communicate it.
- Do you plan to offer an open question time at the end?
- Let the audience know whether or not you will take interruptions during your presentation.

Evidence

Keep the assessment points in mind: match your work against the learning outcomes across the marking grids. Evidence must be real and valid, not inferred.

What students need to produce

- Evaluate your evidence – and evidence your evaluation.
- Use photographs and witness statements to provide evidence.
- Don't copy work from other units: plagiarism of your own work isn't a good idea, and it is easy to identify.
- Document and structure your evidence – don't just include it without organisation.
- Your timescale and word count must be clearly shown.
- You need to provide your work log and diary as evidence.
- Research records and referencing – structure your research and treat it systematically.
- Use a range of sources, without relying too much on websites. Your research should have sufficient breadth and depth, and it should be evidenced and identified. Be judgemental about your use of other people's work.
- Use proper effective referencing: good referencing and bibliographies lead to good scores. Effective referencing allows you to prove that your work has a sound theoretical base.
- Project Progression Record (PPR) – an essential record of your work – must be included, whatever format the outcome of your project takes.

Moderator's hint
Do not confuse the PPR with your plan. A plan is something which is produced before you start, and revisited, modified and updated regularly (and evidence kept of this).
The PPR is completed as you progress, and may link to your plan by modifying the timings of your activities.

You need to show and explain how your project topic builds on your principal learning or how it supports your intended progression pathway.

Skills, techniques and tools

Project management skills

You need to learn effective project management skills and effective techniques and tools to realise the outcome of your project.

- Keep your project on track, to scale and on time. Time management skills are essential.
- Remember that the scope and focus define the EP.
- Monitor your own progress and targets, making use of your supervisor.
- Plan the structure: review it constantly. Thorough planning will prepare you for most pitfalls.
- Control your enthusiasm – if you are researching a topic of personal interest, don't let your interest become sidestepped into over-researching.
- If time is running out, what can you afford to chop or trim? Study the assessment grids – where are the most marks available? If you need to trim your material, do not cut material for which marks are awarded. Remember the following areas are being assessed:
  - Managing a project (12 marks)
  - Using resources (12 marks)
  - Developing and realising a project (24 marks)
  - Reviewing the project (12 marks).

Conduct research on the Internet, refining your search on a search engine. Purposeful research and selection/trimming is essential for Level 3.

Make use of technologies to solve problems: keep plenty of backups of your work. 'Lost data = failure' so don't let this happen.

Moderator's hint
If politicians and senior police officers lose valuable data, they face prison or dismissal. If you lose data, you could fail the Extended Project, so make sure this doesn't happen.

- Make decisions and be critical and flexible to achieve your outcomes.
- Don't just keep everything you research:
  - be selective
  - critically appraise
  - filter
  - discard (or put somewhere safe, just in case).
- Work with others, including your supervisor. If team activities or group work are involved, take responsibility for a realistic chunk of the work or task.
- Manage your own learning: become an expert, independent learner.

Project skills

You will be taught 'project skills'. In this time you can expect to learn the following:

- Techniques to help you select a project topic which is relevant to your study and/or future progression into work or further studies.
- How to focus on a question or some task(s) associated with that topic.
- Writing a project brief which specifies the intended outcome(s) of your project work.
- A range of project management skills and tools which are available to help you.
- Planning your work and, more importantly, your time.
- How to carry out research and make effective use of all the material you find.
- Putting your research findings into practice, and how to evaluate your work at every step.
- Keeping a focus on your intended project outcomes.
- Produce your final project and evaluation, drawing conclusions and reflecting on what you have learned.
- Developing and delivering an effective presentation about your project.

Realising your project

You should then expect to 'do' your project on your own with minimal supervision. Remember that it should be the equivalent, in terms of time and effort spent of it, of half on A level and it will be assessed at A Level (not AS) standards.

- While carrying out your project, you will develop independent learning skills.
- You will become better at making decisions and solving problems as they occur or predicting them before they happen.
- Your work on the project will require initiative and creativity.
- You will develop skills which will help guide your career choice(s).
- You will develop an interest in studying beyond your current scope, possibly linked to future career development.
- The experiences of carrying out the Extended Project will help prepare you for future challenges.
- Your presentation skills and confidence will increase following your project development and completion.
- You will learn how different technologies can help you with every part of the project and your future studies.

> **HOW TO SUCCEED**
>
> Remember that the project must be **your own work**. The Extended Project is about you, whereas other qualifications which you are undertaking are shared by others. Make it something special, and keep it that way.

Problem-solving skills

The assessment criteria for the Extended Project indicates that problem-solving should be assessed where relevant, but it is not difficult to identify problems and issues which you will have been solving, without even realising that you had solved them. So what are the essential and recognisable problem-solving skills?

Consider the following: what if your plans aren't working? Plans are made to show that you have thought about the processes which you intend to work through.

- Changing your mind is allowed, and can offer advantages and disadvantages. If you find your research or progress slowing down, it is quite acceptable to change your plans and start working towards a different type of project outcome.
- Document your changes, and explain/justify your reasons for changing. This is good project management, so keep the evidence.
- Keep focused and don't try to hide your problems as they crop up – make use of them.

> **HOW TO SUCCEED**
>
> Having a 'problem-solving' project can more readily lead to higher grades.

- Analyse everything you do: develop and improve your own learning and performance, and become a self-critical, reflective and independent learner.
- Whatever your topic or focus, maintain a constant argument.
- Develop more skills – planning, research, critical thinking, synthesis, evaluation, and presentation.
- Develop your e-learning skills – embrace new technologies.
- Ensure you have evidence of your evaluation.
- Recommend the 'next step' if the work were to continue

- Self evaluation – how well have you done on all tasks?
  - What could (will) you do to improve?
  - What skills do you need to develop?
  - How can you develop these skills?
- Use and evidence your initiative. Be enterprising.

Summary of learning outcomes for AO4

- Evaluate your outcomes, including your own learning and performance.
- Select and use a range of communication skills and different media to convey and present your evidence outcomes and conclusions.
- Evaluate the project, analyse your project outcomes, draw relevant conclusions.
- Present the outcome to an audience, using it to claim AOs – aim for maximum points and a high grade.

How to be successful

Learning goals

By the end of the chapter you should be able to:

- Realise that the project is assessed on 'skills' not 'content'
- Reflect on feedback from previous project results

At the end of 2008, some of the best Extended Projects (which were marked at higher than 80 per cent and in real conditions would achieve either an A or an A*) were looked at carefully. The following points list the outstanding features of those students' projects.

- Students chose the project for themselves, planned them carefully themselves and translated their initial idea into something that actually worked.
- They showed real organisational skills throughout, as well as enterprise and initiative.
- They responded sensibly to the guidance offered by the supervisor and any expert advice, but avoided the temptation to be spoon-fed and dictated to.
- They used a wide range of resources critically, analysing the information gleaned from those sources and using it to good effect.
- Any problems which arose during the course of the project were dealt with, such as changing formats.
- They demonstrated a wide range of skills.
- Any new skills which needed to be learned were identified in time, learned and successfully used.
- They completed the project on time.
- They carried out in-depth evaluations, showing a high level of insight into how they managed the whole project from beginning to end, and what were the strengths and limitations of the resources at their disposal.
- They took their presentations seriously in order to demonstrate their communication skills, the outcomes and their conclusions, choosing the right format with a good range of supporting evidence.
- They showed a deep and extensive knowledge of the project area of study through their responses to questions.

> **Moderator's hint**
> Note that the focus is on skills, the 'content' part, comes at the very end.

Glossary

Al dente – Italian culinary term referring to pasta which is firm on the teeth. Commonly used to refer to food, particularly vegetables, which my grandmother would say are 'only half cooked', but refers to a culinary skill which leads to the food being cooked, but not tender or mushy.

Assessment Objective (AO) – similar to learning outcome or learning goal.

CPN – critical path network – method of planning and monitoring projects by using diagrams to illustrate activities and durations (*see also* PERT).

Functional skills – defined as the essential skills for life, learning and work. The necessary skills are identified across English, maths and ICT; similar to key skills (and before that 'common skills' or 'transferable skills').

FE - further education – generally colleges and sixth forms, but also training providers and others; usually refers to Level 2 and 3 study, but can include Foundation learning, entry level, etc.

Feedback – a term which is commonly used to refer to any form of cyclical process where information about the result or the output is 'fed back' for comparison with the input of the process.

Gantt chart – a way of representing time on a diagram, allowing projects to be planned involving several activities. (*refer to* http://www.ganttchart.com/Evolution.html; *see also* PERT)

HE – higher education – above Level 3 (HND/Foundation degree, first degree, higher degrees – Masters and PhD).

ICT – Information and communications technology – a bit more than just computing (IT) due to the development of extremely useful communications systems which help us all communicate, wherever we are.

Key skills – defined as the skills which are generally required for success in education, training, work, and life in general. There are 6 areas included in the key skills: communication, application of numbers, ICT, working with others, improving own learning and performance, and problem solving (the last three are generally referred to as the wider key skills).

Learning goal – what you actually intend to learn by carrying out a course of study – the goal of your learning.

Learning outcome – or assessment objective (AO) – similar to learning goal.

OCR – one of the major awarding bodies (exam boards) formed by the merger of three exam boards: Oxford, Cambridge and the Royal College of Arts.

Referencing – a method of identifying the original author of articles which a later author refers to, builds on, or argues against; several styles in use including Harvard and Chicago styles.

PERT – Program [or Project] Evaluation and Review Technique – diagrammatical representation of a planned project with activities and durations, allowing the control of operations with reference to the critical path (*refer to* http://www.netmba.com/operations/project/pert/; *see also* CPN or Network diagrams).

Plagiarism – using someone's work and passing it off as your own; theft of work, design or copyright.

PLTS – Personal Learning and Thinking Skills – an assessment framework developed to suit the requirements of industry. There are 6 PLTS which can be used to describe the way we individually learn and think: independent enquirers, creative thinkers, reflective learners, team workers, self managers, effective participators.

Presentation – a demonstration of communication skills, which can take the form of a stand-up talk using presentation equipment (PowerPoint, OHPs, etc.), a display (wall mounted or on a table), a poster, a series of photographs with explanations, etc.

Progression – a term used to refer to moving on to the next level, e.g. from school to sixth form or college, work, or apprenticeship, then to university, work, management, etc.

Project format (or type) – there are five project formats or types – design, performance, report, dissertation or artefact.

SMART – when referring to target setting. SMART targets should be specific, measurable, achievable, realistic, time bound (or time related).

UCAS – Universities and Colleges Admissions Service – an organisation through which all applicants to higher education should apply.

URL – uniform resource locator – a web site or web page location; web address – e.g. http://www.blahblahblah.com.